Michael N. Kuryla L. Cox

Laura P. Bitonte SK

Woodie E James

AIRCRAFT
OF WORLD WAR II

AIRCRAFT
OF WORLD WAR II

Mike Sharpe

MBI Publishing Company

This edition first published in 2000 by MBI Publishing
Company, 729 Prospect Avenue, PO Box 1, Osceola, WI
54020-0001 USA

The information in this book is true and complete to the best
of our knowledge. All recommendations are made without any
guarantee on the part of the author or publisher, who also
disclaim any liability incurred in connection with the use of this
data or specified details.

We recognize that some words, model names and
designations, for example, mentioned herein are the property
of the trademark holder. We use them for identification
purposes only. This is not an official publication.

MBI Publishing Company books are also available at discounts
in bulk quantity for industrial or sales-promotional use. For
details write to Special Sales Manager at Motorbooks
International Wholesalers & Distributors, 729 Prospect
Avenue, PO Box 1, Osceola, WI 54020-0001 USA.

Library of Congress Cataloging-in-Publication Data Available.

ISBN 0-7603-0934-5

Printed in Hong Kong

Editorial and design
Brown Partworks Limited
8 Chapel Place
Rivington Street
London
EC2A 3DQ
UK

Editor: Chris Westhorp
Picture research: Antony Shaw
Design: Spencer Holbrook
Production: Matt Weyland

Picture Credits
All photographs The Robert Hunt Library except:
TRH Pictures: 94

CONTENTS

ARADO Ar 234 BLITZ

SPECIFICATIONS

ARADO Ar 234 BLITZ

Manufacturer: **Arado Flugzeugwerke**	*Crew:* **One**
Type: **Reconnaissance/Bomber**	*Powerplant:* **2 or 4 x Jumo turbojets**
Length: **12.65m (41ft 5.5in)**	*Armament:* **2 x MG 151 cannon**
Span: **14.40m (47ft 3.25in)**	*Bomb load:* **1500kg (3300lb)**
Height: **4.3m (14ft 1.25in)**	*First flight:* **15 June 1943**
Maximum speed: **780km/h (485mph)**	*Initial climb:* **Not Available**
Service ceiling: **16,370m (36,090ft)**	*Weight (empty):* **4800kg (10,580lb)**
Range: **2000km (1243 miles)**	*Weight (loaded):* **16,370m (36,090ft)**

The *Blitz* (Lightning) was the only turbojet-powered bomber to achieve operational status in World War II and is a milestone in military aviation's development. Its evolution dates from a 1940 requirement issued by the German Air Ministry (Luftfahrtministerium) for a fast reconnaissance aeroplane. An intensive programme of design and development resulted in no fewer than 18 prototypes, featuring a powerplant of two Junkers 004 or four BMW 003 turbojets, provision for rocket-assisted take-off units, a cabin with or without pressurization and an ejection seat, and a clumsy combination of a drop-away trolley for take-off and extendible skids for landing. A few of these prototypes were used from July 1944 by the reconnaissance units (Aufklärungsgruppe).

The production Ar 234B was intended for the reconnaissance bomber role with hardpoints under the fuselage and two engine nacelles for a 500kg (1100lb) bombload and utilized retractable tricycle landing gear in place of the trolley, an arrangement pioneered in the Ar 234 V9 prototype. Some 210 Ar 234B-1 reconnaissance aircraft with drop tanks in place of bombs and Ar 234B-2 reconnaissance bombers were built. The type entered service in September 1944, and was complemented by just 14 examples of the Ar 234C with the revised powerplant of four BMW 109-003A-1 turbojets.

ARADO Ar 95

Walter Blume designed the Arado Ar 95 in 1935 for the coastal patrol, reconnaissance and light attack role. It was a two-seat biplane with metallic fuselage and rear-folding wings. The wings had a metal structure, with the top one skinned in metal and the lower one in canvas. The prototype (Ar-95 V1) first flew during 1937, fitted with a Junkers Jumo V12 engine of 455kW (610hp).

Several prototypes tested successive modifications such as enlarged tail surfaces, a closed cockpit and a change to the 630kW (845hp) radial BMW 132 engine. The Ar-95 V3 was a three-seat version and the Ar-95 V4 had a fixed and spatted wheeled undercarriage. While the prototypes were still being tested, a pre-production run was started and several served in Spain with the Condor Legion. A small number were later in front-line Luftwaffe service early in the war before being relegated to training duties. The Ar-95A version had the BMW 132DC engine of 657kW (880hp) and a variable-pitch three-bladed propeller. The armament was a single fixed forward-firing MG15, mounted on the fuselage to fire through the propeller, and another MG15 on a flexible mounting to the rear. Under-fuselage it could carry a 700kg (1540lb) torpedo or a 375kg (825lb) bomb; under each wing 50kg (110lb) bombs. Chile bought six – three Ar 95A floatplanes and three wheeled-version Ar 95Bs.

SPECIFICATIONS

ARADO Ar 95A-1

Manufacturer: **Arado Flugzeugwerke**	Crew: **Two**
Type: **Coast Patrol, Light Attack**	Powerplant: **1 x BMW 132 radial**
Length: **11.10m (36ft 5in)**	Armament: **2 x 7.92mm MG15**
Span: **12.5m (41ft)**	Bomb load: **800kg (1760lb)**
Height: **3.60m (11ft 9.75in)**	First flight: **1937**
Maximum speed: **310km/h (193mph)**	Initial climb: **Not Available**
Service ceiling: **7300m (23,945ft)**	Weight (empty): **2450kg (5402lb)**
Range: **1100km (683 miles)**	Weight (loaded): **3560kg (7870lb)**

BLOHM UND VOSS Bv 141

SPECIFICATIONS

BLOHM UND VOSS Bv 141

Manufacturer: **Blohm und Voss**	Crew: **Three**
Type: **Tactical Reconnaissance**	Powerplant: **1 x BMW 801A radial**
Length: **13.95m (45ft 9.25in)**	Armament: **4 x 7.92mm MG**
Span: **17.46m (57ft 3.5in)**	Bomb load: **200kg (441lb)**
Height: **3.60m (11ft 9.75in)**	First flight: **25 February 1938**
Maximum speed: **438km/h (272mph)**	Initial climb: **Not Available**
Service ceiling: **10,000m (32,810ft)**	Weight (empty): **4700kg (10,362lb)**
Range: **1900km (1181 miles)**	Weight (loaded): **6100kg (13,448lb)**

In 1937 the Luftfahrtministerium (German Air Ministry) issued a requirement for a single-engined three-seat tactical reconnaissance aeroplane, drawing submissions from Focke Wulf in the form of its Fw 189, and Blohm und Voss's Bv 141 design. Much emphasis was placed on the need for good visibility, and in response the Bv 141 had a highly unusual asymmetric layout with the fully glazed crew nacelle offset to starboard of the centreline and a boom (carrying the engine at its front and a tail unit at its rear) offset to port.

The first of three prototypes flew in February 1938, and were evaluated at Erprobungstelle Rechlin with sufficient success to extract an order from the ministry for five Bv 141A-0 pre-production aircraft. Evaluation was completed successfully, but the type had poor performance as a result of its use of the 645kW (865hp) BMW 132N engine and so the next five aircraft were redesigned Bv 141B-0 machines with an uprated powerplant as well as a strengthened structure and a revised tail unit. These aircraft were used by the Aufklärungschule 1 for service trials over the UK and the USSR from the autumn of 1941, but there were development delays because of persistent hydraulic problems and the programme was ended in 1943.

DORNIER Do 17

Designed as a fast mailplane (with single-fin tail surfaces) for Deutsche Lufthansa and first flown in 1934, the Do 17 was rejected by the airline and then developed by Dornier as a high-speed bomber with twin vertical tail surfaces. The aircraft entered service in early 1937, gaining the nickname "The Flying Pencil" on account of its slender rear fuselage. The first two military variants were the Do 17E-1 and Do 17F-1 for the high-speed bomber and long-range photo-reconnaissance roles respectively, the latter with additional fuel and the internal bomb bay revised to carry two cameras. The two types offered good performance and adequate all-round capabilities for their day, but by 1939 were obsolescent.

Progressive development led to the Do 17M/P medium bomber/reconnaissance aircraft and Do 17S/U reconnaissance/pathfinder types with liquid-cooled engines and a redesigned forward fuselage. The definitive model was the radial-engined Do 17Z of which 522 were built in three variants: the Do 17Z-1 with a 500kg (1102lb) bomb load, Do 17Z-2 with an uprated powerplant and load, and Do 17Z-3 reconnaissance bomber. Conversions included the Do 17Z-4 dual-control trainer, Do 17Z-5 maritime reconnaissance, Do 17Z-6 long-range night-fighter with the nose of the Ju Ju 88C-2, and Do 17Z-10 night-fighter with a redesigned nose.

SPECIFICATIONS

DORNIER Do 17

Manufacturer: **Dornier-Werke GmbH**	Crew: **Four**
Type: **medium bomber**	Powerplant: **2 x BMW Bramo radials**
Length: **15.80m (51ft 9.67in)**	Armament: **1 or 2 7.92mm MG**
Span: **18.00m (59ft 0.5in)**	Bomb load: **1000kg (2205lb)**
Height: **4.60m (15ft 1in)**	First flight: **Autumn 1934**
Maximum speed: **410km/h (255mph)**	Initial climb: **Not Available**
Service ceiling: **8200m (26,905ft)**	Weight (empty): **5200kg (11,464lb)**
Range: **1500km (932 miles)**	Weight (loaded): **8590kg (18,937lb)**

DORNIER Do 18

SPECIFICATIONS

DORNIER Do 18

Manufacturer: **Dornier-Werke GmbH**	Crew: **5/6**
Type: **Maritime Reconnaisance**	Powerplant: **2 x Jumo 205D diesels**
Length: **19.37m (63ft 7in)**	Armament: **1 x cannon, 1 x MG**
Span: **23.70m (77ft 9.25in)**	Bomb load: **100kg (220lb)**
Height: **5.32m (17ft 5.5in)**	First flight: **15 March 1935**
Maximum speed: **267km/h (166mph)**	Initial climb: **114m (374ft) per min**
Service ceiling: **4200m (13,780ft)**	Weight (empty): **5980kg (13,183lb)**
Range: **3500km (2175 miles)**	Weight (loaded): **10,800kg (23,809lb)**

The Do 18 was originally produced as a trans-Atlantic mail carrier to supersede the Dornier Wal 33 (from 1934 Do 15) in service with Deutsche Lufthansa on its South Atlantic routes, and later used as a medium-range maritime reconnaissance type by the Luftwaffe. The first of four prototypes made its maiden flight in March 1935, one of them being used for an experimental crossing of the North Atlantic. The twin-Junkers Jumo 205 diesels were mounted in tandem above the wing centre section, itself carried on a semi-circular hull with characteristic Dornier under-surface and lateral sponsons, and strengthened for catapulting (most German warships were equipped with catapults for mounting aircraft – vital for long-range reconnaissance).

Only six civil flying boats were completed, the majority of the approximately 148 production boats going to the military for service from 1938. The primary military variants were the Do 18D (three sub-variants to a total of about 75 machines) with 447.5kW (600hp) Junkers Jumo 205D Diesel engines, the Do 18G improved Do 18D with revised armament and provision for RATO units, and the Do 18H six-seat trainer. Do 18G and Do-18H production was 71 flying boats, and many Do 18G machines were converted to Do 18N standard as air-sea rescue flying boats.

DORNIER Do 217

The Do 217 was Dornier's response to a 1937 requirement for a long-range warplane optimized for the heavy level and dive-bombing roles, though later it was used in a variety of roles, even as a test bed for missile development. The Do 217 was in essence a scaled-up Do 215 version of the Do 17, and first flew in August 1938. The first operational model was the Do 217E of which some 800 aircraft were built in Do 217E-0 to Do 217E-4 sub-variants with BMW 801 radial engines. These were followed by the Do 217J, a night-fighter developed from the E which was structurally similar except for a redesigned solid armoured nose with a forward-firing armament comprising four 20mm MG FF cannon. It proved to be a potent aircraft.

Other variants were the Do 217K night bomber distinguished by a revised and unstepped nose, and finally the Do 217M development of the Do 217K with DB 603 inverted-Vee engines. Prototype and pre-production variants were the Do 217C bomber, Do 217P high-altitude reconnaissance, and Do 217R missile launching aircraft. There were also five Do 217E and two Do 217K sub-variants, notably the E-5 and K-2 (which had longer span wings), which were armed with Hs 293 anti-ship missiles and Fritz-X 1400 radio-corrected armour-piercing bombs respectively.

SPECIFICATIONS

DORNIER Do 217

Manufacturer: **Dornier-Werke GmbH**	Crew: **Four**
Type: **Heavy Bomber**	Powerplant: **2 x BMW 801ML radials**
Length: **18.20m (59ft 8.5in)**	Armament: **1 x cannon, 5 x MG**
Span: **19.00m (62ft 4in)**	Bomb load: **4000kg (8818lb)**
Height: **5.03m (16ft 6in)**	First flight: **August 1938**
Maximum speed: **515km/h (320mph)**	Initial climb: **216m (708ft) per min**
Service ceiling: **9000m (29,530ft)**	Weight (empty): **10,535kg (23,225lb)**
Range: **2800km (1740 miles)**	Weight (loaded): **16,465kg (36,299lb)**

FIESELER Fi 156 STORCH

SPECIFICATIONS

FIESELER Fi 156 STORCH

Manufacturer: **Gerhard Fieseler Werke**	Crew: **One**
Type: **Communications**	Powerplant: **1 x Argus inverted-Vee**
Length: **9.90m (32ft 5.75in)**	Armament: **1 x 7.92mm MG**
Span: **14.25m (46ft 9in)**	Bomb load: **Not Available**
Height: **3.05m (10ft)**	First flight: **March 1936**
Maximum speed: **175km/h (109mph)**	Initial climb: **286m (937ft) per min**
Service ceiling: **5200m (17,060ft)**	Weight (empty): **940kg (2072lb)**
Range: **1015km (631 miles)**	Weight (loaded): **1320kg (2910lb)**

The Fieseler Fi 156 *Storch* (Stork) was designed in response to a 1935 requirement issued by the Luftfahrtministerium for an army cooperation, casualty evacuation and liaison aeroplane. In prototype form it first flew in the spring of 1936 and entered service the following year. The ungainly but highly effective "Stork" was one of the most remarkable aircraft produced by the German aero industry during the Nazi regime. By incorporating innovative high-lift devices that he pioneered on pre-war acrobatic types, Gerhard Fieseler produced an aircraft with outstanding capability. This is borne out by some remarkable statistics: the Fi 156 Storch could take-off in 65m (213ft), land in 20m (66ft) and virtually hover in a 40km/h (25mph) wind without any loss of control.

Hitler's personal pilot used the exceptional STOL capability to land on an Alpine hotel terrace during the daring mountainside rescue of Benito Mussolini. Production totalled about 2900 aircraft, and the main variants were the initial, unarmed Fi 156A model, Fi-156C armed model in four main sub-variants, and Fi 156D air ambulance model in two sub-variants. The aircraft was held in high regard on both sides; at least three Allied generals are known to have used captured aircraft as their personal transportation.

FOCKE WULF Fw 189

Despite its unusual appearance, which brought more than a few words of scepticism from conservative Luftwaffe pilots, the Fw 189 *Uhu* (Owl) was extremely effective in its intended role of army cooperation and short-range reconnaissance. It was only one of two such aircraft produced for the Luftwaffe – somewhat strangely considering it was designed primarily as a tactical air force for the support of the army. The prototype first flew in July 1938 – none of the subsequent prototype aircraft were alike – yet it was unknown by the Allies until it was disclosed in 1941 as the "Flying Eye" of German armies.

The aircraft was a twin-boom monoplane that accommodated the crew in an extensively glazed central nacelle. Service deliveries began in late 1940, and on the Eastern Front the aircraft performed beyond all expectations, retaining its superb handling and showing a remarkable ability to withstand damage and poor weather. Production totalled 848, excluding the 16 prototype and pre-production aircraft. The main model was the Fw 189A, produced in sub-variants such as the Fw 189A-1, Fw 189A-2 with twin rather than single defensive machine guns, Fw 189A-3 dual-control trainer, and Fw 189A-4 tactical support model with ventral armour and armed with a 20mm cannon rather than machine guns in the wing roots.

SPECIFICATIONS

FOCKE WULF Fw 189 UHU

Manufacturer: **Focke Wulf Flugzeugbau**	Crew: **Three**
Type: **Reconnaissance**	Powerplant: **2 x Argus As 410A-1**
Length: **12.03m (39ft 5.5in)**	Armament: **4 x 7.92mm MG**
Span: **18.40m (60ft 4.5in)**	Bomb load: **not available**
Height: **3.10m (10ft 2in)**	First flight: **July 1938**
Maximum speed: **350km/h (217mph)**	Initial climb: **485m (1590ft) per min**
Service ceiling: **7300m (23,950ft)**	Weight (empty): **3245kg (7154lb)**
Range: **670km (416 miles)**	Weight (loaded): **4170kg (9193lb)**

FOCKE WULF Fw 190

SPECIFICATIONS

FOCKE WULF Fw 190

Manufacturer: **Focke Wulf Flugzeugbau**	Crew: **One**
Type: **Single-seat Fighter**	Powerplant: **1 x BMW 801D-2 radial**
Length: **8.80m (28ft 10.5in)**	Armament: **4 x cannon, 2 x MG**
Span: **10.50m (34ft 5.5in)**	Bomb load: **not available**
Height: **3.95m (12ft 11.5in)**	First flight: **1 June 1939**
Maximum speed: **3.95m (12ft 11.5in)**	Initial climb: **863m (2830ft) per min**
Service ceiling: **10,600m (34,775ft)**	Weight (empty): **2900kg (6393lb)**
Range: **800km (497 miles)**	Weight (loaded): **3980kg (8770lb)**

This outstanding aircraft was in fact the only new fighter design to enter service with the Luftwaffe during the war. The prototype flew in June 1939 and after an intensive development programme in which both vee and radial engines were trialled, the Fw 190A entered production with a BMW 801 radial engine. The 40 Fw 190A-0 pre-production aircraft were followed by 100 Fw 190A-1 fighters, and the type entered service in the autumn of 1940. Although well known to the Allies prior to the war, the Fw 190 caused a nasty shock when it was first encountered over France in May 1941. It was light, manoeuvrable, fast, powerfully armed and immensely strong.

The A-1 was followed into service by the longer-span Fw 190A-2 with heavier armament, the Fw 190A-3 fighter-bomber with revised armament and Fw 190A-4 fighter-bombers with a methanol/water power boost system. There followed a profusion of different versions, and although the aircraft was substantially better than virtually all of the versions of the Spitfire, the Fw 190 never supplanted the Messerschmitt Bf 109 in production. As development of the aircraft progressed it was used increasingly in the fighter-bomber role and gained heavier armament, strengthened landing gear and numerous different engine fitments.

FOCKE WULF Fw 200

The Condor was designed as a transatlantic airliner for the German airline Deutsche Lufthansa. It first flew in prototype form during July 1937 and subsequently set up impressive record flights to New York and Tokyo, attracting export orders from Denmark, Brazil, Finland and Japan. The latter country ordered one aircraft for use as a long-range reconnaissance platform, and the resulting prototype attracted the attentions of the Luftwaffe, which put the aircraft into production.

The first of 259 Fw 200C military aircraft entered service in September 1939, and after the capitulation of France in 1940 they flew from bases along the Atlantic coast, searching for Allied convoys in the North Atlantic and then either attacking them directly with bombs and missiles or vectoring in packs of German U-boats. So effective were they in this role that Prime Minister Churchill labelled the Condor "the scourge of the Atlantic". A few aircraft were used as VIP transports (notably by Hitler and Himmler), but the majority of the machines were long-range reconnaissance bombers in seven sub-variants, some of which spawned their own sub-variants with different armament-fits, radar-fits and provision for missile-carriage and -guidance, as well as stripped-down forms for special transport tasks.

SPECIFICATIONS

FOCKE WULF Fw 200

Manufacturer: **Focke Wulf Flugzeugbau**	Crew: **Five**
Type: **Maritime Recon' Bomber**	Powerplant: **4 x BMW-Bramo 323R-2**
Length: **23.46m (76ft 11.5in)**	Armament: **1 x cannon, 4 x MG**
Span: **32.84m (107ft 8in)**	Bomb load: **2100kg (4630lb)**
Height: **6.30m (20ft 8in)**	First flight: **not given**
Maximum speed: **360km/h (224mph)**	Initial climb: **not available**
Service ceiling: **6000m (19,685ft)**	Weight (empty): **12,950kg (28,549lb)**
Range: **4440km (2759 miles)**	Weight (loaded): **22,700kg (50,044lb)**

GOTHA Go 242 and 244

SPECIFICATIONS

GOTHA Go 242 AND 244

Manufacturer: **Gotha Waggonfabrik**	Crew: **Two**
Type: **Troop Transporter**	Powerplant: **2 x Gnome-Rhône radial**
Length: **15.80m (51ft 10.25in)**	Armament: **4 x 7.92mm MG**
Span: **24.50m (80ft 4.5in)**	Bomb load: **Not Available**
Height: **4.60m (15ft 1in)**	First flight: **Not Given**
Maximum speed: **290km/h (180mph)**	Initial climb: **270m (885ft) per min**
Service ceiling: **7650m (25,100ft)**	Weight (empty): **5225kg (11,517lb)**
Range: **740km (460 miles)**	Weight (loaded): **7800kg (17,196lb)**

Well known as a producer of bomber aircraft for the German Air Service during World War I, Gotha re-entered aircraft production in 1936 and after the outbreak of war devoted its attentions to the design and manufacture of military aircraft. The most successful of its wartime designs was the Go 242, a high-wing twin-boom monoplane with a central nacelle that could accommodate 23 fully equipped troops. Introduced into service in 1942, the Go 242 subsequently became the Luftwaffe's standard transport glider, with deliveries totalling 1526 Go 242A and Go 242B gliders with skid and wheeled landing gear respectively.

Typically, the aircraft were towed by Ju 52 or He 111 aircraft, and were used during the daring airborne invasion of Crete in May 1941. The Go 242 was designed with a view to the installation of engines, and its success paved the way for the Go 244, which was powered with French engines. Deliveries totalled 174 aircraft, including 133 converted Go 242B gliders. Of this latter type there were five versions: the Go 244B-1 freighter with torsion-bar shock absorption, Go 244B-2 freighter with wider track main units and oleo shock absorption, Go 244B-3 and B-4 paratroop transport versions of the Go 244B-1 and B-2, and Go 244B-5 with dual controls and balanced rudders.

HEINKEL He 60

One of the last of the many floatplanes designed by Ernst Heinkel was the He 60, a two-seat biplane powered by a BMW vee engine. This was intended for catapult operations from the decks of the larger German warships, and first flew in 1933 in prototype form. The 492kW (660hp) BMW VI engine was subsequently replaced in the second He 60B prototype by a 559kW (750hp) version of the same engine, but this offered no significant improvement and was not adopted for subsequent aircraft. The third He 60c prototype had catapult launching equipment and underwent a series of trials that confirmed its suitability for operational use.

The first production He 60B aircraft entered service with training units in 1933 and as the programme of rebuilding Germany's navy accelerated, the type was selected for service aboard German battle cruisers and cruisers. In 1934 an improved version (He 60C) was introduced. The aircraft saw extensive service in the Spanish Civil War, where it performed well. By the time that war had broken out in Europe at the beginning of September 1939, however, the He 60 was fast becoming obsolete and it was soon relegated to training duties only, although German maritime reconnaissance units based in Greece and Crete continued to operate the He 60 until 1943.

SPECIFICATIONS

HEINKEL He 60

Manufacturer: **Ernst Heinkel A.G**	Crew: **Two**
Type: **Reconnaissance Seaplane**	Powerplant: **1 x BMW VI 6.0ZU**
Length: **11.48m (37ft 8in)**	Armament: **2 x MG**
Span: **13.5m (44ft 3in)**	Bomb load: **None**
Height: **N/A**	First flight: **1933**
Maximum speed: **225km/h (140mph)**	Initial climb: **N/A**
Service ceiling: **5000m (16,400ft)**	Weight (empty): **N/A**
Range: **720km (447 miles)**	Weight (loaded): **N/A**

HEINKEL He 111

SPECIFICATIONS

HEINKEL HE 111

Manufacturer: Ernst Heinkel A.G.	**Crew:** 4/5
Type: Medium Bomber	**Powerplant:** 2 x Junkers Jumo 211F-2
Length: 16.40m (53ft 9.5in)	**Armament:** 7 x 7.92mm MG
Span: 22.60m (74ft 1.75in)	**Bomb load:** 2500kg (5511lb)
Height: 3.40m (13ft 1.5in)	**First flight:** 24 February 1935
Maximum speed: 405km/h (252mph)	**Initial climb:** 170m (558ft) per min
Service ceiling: 8500m (27,890ft)	**Weight (empty):** 8680kg (19,136lb)
Range: 1930km (1199 miles)	**Weight (loaded):** 14,000kg (30,865lb)

The Heinkel He 111 was the natural twin-engined outgrowth of the Heinkel 70 bomber used to such great effect in Spain. Although revealed to the world as a civil airliner, it was designed for bombing. Powered by twin BMW VI engines, it could carry 1000kg (2205lb) of bombs stowed nose-up in eight cells in the centre section. In 1937 some similar machines flew secret reconnaissance missions over Britain, France and the Soviet Union in the guise of airliners, and in the same year the He 111B-1 entered service with the Luftwaffe. In February 1937 operations began with the Condor Legion in Spain, where its seeming invincibility led many to become complacent.

The 300 He 111B-1s were followed by 190 He 111E bombers with Junkers Jumo 211 engines. The next significant model, in spring 1939, was the He 111P with the asymmetric fully glazed nose typical of all subsequent models. Some 400 aircraft were built in six sub-variants (He 111P-1 to He 111P-6). The definitive model was the He 111H (6150 built in 23 sub-variants). Development was characterized by a progressively uprated powerplant, increased fuel capacity, improved defensive and offensive armament, additional armour protection and provision for use in alternative roles: anti-shipping, pathfinding, missile platform, paratroop-delivery and glider-towing.

HEINKEL He 112

One of the first requirements issued under the Nazis by the rapidly expanded Reichsluftfahrtministerium was a specification for a monoplane fighter to replace the Arado 68 and Heinkel 51. Designed by a Heinkel team under Walter Günthers (who was also responsible for the He 70), the He 112 was Heinkel's entry to the competition.

The Heinkel was comparatively advanced, and the first of an eventual 12 prototypes flew in the summer of 1935. During the programme a number of powerplant, fuselage, wing and tail unit configurations were investigated. The Luftwaffe then selected the Bf 109, but the German Air Ministry was sufficiently impressed with the Heinkel to order 43 He 112B-0 pre-production aircraft that operated with a fighter wing during 1938. Seventeen of the aircraft were sent to Spain to fight in the Civil War (not as part of the Condor Legion, but flown instead by civilian volunteers), after which the 15 survivors were passed to the Spanish Nationalist forces. Of the others, Germany sold 13 each to Japan and Romania, the latter subsequently also acquiring 11 of the 13 He 112B-1 production aircraft for service up to 1942, notably during the invasion of the Soviet Union in June 1941. Hungary also acquired a few aircraft.

SPECIFICATIONS

HEINKEL He 112

Manufacturer: **Ernst Heinkel A.G.**	Crew: **One**
Type: **Fighter, Ground-Attack**	Powerplant: **1 x Junkers Jumo 210Ea**
Length: **9.30m (30ft 6in)**	Armament: **2 x cannon, 2 x MG**
Span: **9.10m (29ft 10.25in)**	Bomb load: **60kg (132lb)**
Height: **3.85m (12ft 7.5in)**	First flight: **September 1935**
Maximum speed: **510km/h (317mph)**	Initial climb: **700m (2,300ft) per min**
Service ceiling: **8500m (27,890ft)**	Weight (empty): **1620kg (3571lb)**
Range: **1100km (683 miles)**	Weight (loaded): **2250kg (4960lb)**

HENSCHEL Hs 126

SPECIFICATIONS

HENSCHEL Hs 126

Manufacturer: **Henschel Flugzeug-Werke**	Crew: **Two**
Type: **Reconnaissance**	Powerplant: **1 x BMW-Bramo 323A-1**
Length: **10.85m (35ft 7in)**	Armament: **2 x 7.92mm MG**
Span: **14.50m (47ft 6.75in)**	Bomb load: **150kg (331lb)**
Height: **3.75m (12ft 3.5in)**	First flight: **autumn 1936**
Maximum speed: **355km/h (221mph)**	Initial climb: **not given**
Service ceiling: **8230m (27,000ft)**	Weight (empty): **2032kg (4480lb)**
Range: **720km (447 miles)**	Weight (loaded): **3270kg (7209lb)**

A development of the earlier Hs 122 trainer and light reconnaissance aircraft of 1934, the Hs 126 provided the Germans with the bulk of their battlefield reconnaissance capability in World War II. It gained a new wing, cantilever main landing gear and a canopy over the pilot's cockpit, which were fitted to an Hs 122 airframe to produce the Junkers Jumo 210-powered prototype that first flew in autumn 1936. This was followed by two development aircraft powered by a Bramo Fafnir 323A-1 and 10 Hs 126A-0 pre-production, some of which were evaluated by German forces fighting alongside the Nationalists in the Spanish Civil War.

These aircraft paved the way for about 800 examples of the two production variants, the first of which entered service during 1938 with Aufklärungsgruppe 35. These models were the Hs 126A-1 with the 656kW (880hp) BMW 132Dc radial engine, and the Hs 126B-1 fitted with a different engine. The Hs 126 served in a front-line role through to 1942, when they began to be replaced by the Focke Wulf Fw 189, and were thereafter relegated to the glider-towing and night harassment roles, the latter with light bomb loads in regions such as the Baltic and Balkans. The Greek Air Force also received 16 examples of the type, which continued in service beyond the end of World War II.

HENSCHEL Hs 129

Designed by Henschel in response to a requirement in spring 1937 for a twin-engine ground-attack aircraft, to provide close air support for ground forces, that could carry at least two 20mm cannon and extensive protection, the Hs 129 was a cantilever low-wing monoplane of all-metal construction and it first flew in spring 1939 with two 347kW (465hp) Argus As 410 inverted-Vee engines. Poor performance hampered development, which was further hindered when the Luftwaffe pilots who tested the prototypes complained about poor fields of vision and sluggish handling. This forced Henschel to undertake a radical series of improvements that resulted in the Hs 129B-1.

In April 1942 this type entered service with captured French radial engines. It was still underpowered, and the engines were both unreliable and vulnerable, but the demands of the Eastern Front resulted in the delivery of 843 Hs 129Bs. The Hs 129B-2, introduced in 1943, incorporated provision for under-fuselage attachments for anti-tank weapons. Sub-variants had cannons whose installation meant the deletion of the machine guns to provide room for the cannon's ammunition, and some 25 Hs 129B-2 warplanes were adapted on the production line with a 75mm BK 7,5 (converted PaK 40L) anti-tank gun in a jettisonable under-fuselage pack.

SPECIFICATIONS

HENSCHEL Hs 129

Manufacturer: **Henschel Flugzeug-Werke**	Crew: **One**
Type: **Close-Support, Anti-Tank**	Powerplant: **2 x Gnome-Rhòne radial**
Length: **9.75m (31ft 11.75in)**	Armament: **2 x cannon, 2 x MG**
Span: **14.20m (46ft 7in)**	Bomb load: **450kg (992lb)**
Height: **3.25m (10ft 8in)**	First flight: **Spring 1939**
Maximum speed: **407km/h (253mph)**	Initial climb: **486m (1595ft) per min**
Service ceiling: **9000m (29,530ft)**	Weight (empty): **4020kg (8862lb)**
Range: **560km (348 miles)**	Weight (loaded): **5250kg (11,574lb)**

JUNKERS Ju 52

SPECIFICATIONS

JUNKERS Ju 52

Manufacturer: **Junkers Flugzeug**	**Crew:** **Three**
Type: **Transport**	**Powerplant:** **3 x BMW 132T-2 radial**
Length: **18.90m (62ft)**	**Armament:** **4 x 7.92mm MG**
Span: **29.20m (95ft 10in)**	**Bomb load:** **Not Available**
Height: **4.52m (14ft 10in)**	**First flight:** **13 October 1930**
Maximum speed: **286km/h (178mph)**	**Initial climb:** **171m (562ft) per min**
Service ceiling: **5900m (19,360ft)**	**Weight (empty):** **6500kg (14,328lb)**
Range: **1305km (811 miles)**	**Weight (loaded):** **11,030kg (24,317lb)**

The "Tante Ju" (Auntie Ju) was the main workhorse of the Luftwaffe transport units for the duration of the war. It was intended as a replacement for the highly successful W 33 and W 34 transports of 1927, and planned from that time as an enlarged version of the same basic design concept with the stressed, corrugated metal skin characteristic of Junkers aircraft. It first flew in prototype form during October 1930 with one 541kW (725hp) BMW VII Vee engine. The Ju 52a to Ju 52d initial production models for the civil market differed only in the type of engine used, but with the Ju 52/3m a three-engined powerplant was introduced for greater payload and performance. Most early Ju 52/3m versions were 15- to 17-seat passenger airliners which sold all over the world, at one time making up 75 per cent of the Lufthansa fleet.

In 1935 the Ju 52/3mg3e bomber, with manually aimed MG 15s in a dorsal cockpit and ventral dustbin, and a bomb load of 1500kg (3307lb) equipped the first Luftwaffe bombing squadron, but nearly all of the 4850 aircraft built – the vast majority of them to meet military orders in variants between the Ju 52/3m ge and the Ju 52/3mg14e – were equipped as troop transports, freighters and casualty evacuation aircraft. During World War II it was used in every theatre through to May 1945.

JUNKERS Ju 87

Newsreels of Ju 87 Stuka dive-bombers peeling off to begin their near vertical attacks are some of the most familiar images of the war. The Ju 87 was planned as a Stuka (short for Sturzkampfluzeug, or "dive-bomber") a name that became synonymous with the type, to provide 'flying artillery' to support the armoured forces that would spearhead Germany's Blitzkrieg (lightning war) tactics, and is forever associated with the success of that strategy early in the war. The aircraft first flew in 1935 with twin vertical tail surfaces and a British Rolls-Royce (RR) Kestrel engine, but was then developed into the Ju 87A initial production model (200 aircraft) with a single vertical surface, the 507kW (680hp) Junkers Jumo 210 inverted-Vee engine, trousered landing gear (to improve the aerodynamic efficiency of the no-retracting undercarriage) and a crutch to swing the bomb away from the fuselage before release.

The Ju 87A entered service in spring 1937 but was soon supplanted by the Ju 87B-1, which had a much uprated powerplant. In Poland the Stuka proved devastating; less than a year later its vulnerability was exposed over southern England. Many sub-variants were produced until 1944; from 1942 to 1945 its main work was close-support and attacking armour on the Eastern Front, although it was also used as a transport and glider tug.

SPECIFICATIONS

JUNKERS Ju 87

Manufacturer: **Junkers Flugzeug**	Crew: **Two**
Type: **Dive-Bomber**	Powerplant: **1 x Junkers Jumo 211Da**
Length: **1.10m (36ft 5in)**	Armament: **3 x 7.92mm MG**
Span: **13.80m (45ft 3.33in)**	Bomb load: **1000kg (2205lb)**
Height: **4.01m (13ft 2in)**	First flight: **November 1935**
Maximum speed: **383km/h (238mph)**	Initial climb: **462m (1515ft) per min**
Service ceiling: **8000m (26,245ft)**	Weight (empty): **2710kg (5974lb)**
Range: **790km (491 miles)**	Weight (loaded): **4340kg (9568lb)**

JUNKERS Ju 88

SPECIFICATIONS

JUNKERS Ju 88

Manufacturer: **Junkers Flugzeug**	Crew: **Four**
Type: **High-Speed Bomber**	Powerplant: **2 x Junkers Jumo 211J**
Length: **14.40m (47ft 2.75in)**	Armament: **7 x 7.92mm MG**
Span: **20m (65ft 7.5in)**	Bomb load: **2500kg (5511lb)**
Height: **4.85m (15ft 11in)**	First flight: **21 December 1936**
Maximum speed: **470km/h (292mph)**	Initial climb: **235m (770ft) per min**
Service ceiling: **8200m (26,900ft)**	Weight (empty): **9860kg (21,737lb)**
Range: **2730km (1696 miles)**	Weight (loaded): **14,000kg (30,865lb)**

Probably no other aircraft in history has been developed in so many different forms for so many purposes as the Ju 88, with the possible exception of Britain's Mosquito. The Ju 88 was flown in 1936 as a civil prototype, and it remained of vital importance to Germany throughout the war. After a frantic design process led by two Americans well versed in modern stressed skin construction, it was transformed into a heavier, slower and more capacious high-speed level- and dive-bomber of the type just then entering service when war broke out. Structurally the aircraft was excellent, combining a large internal fuel capacity with great load-carrying capability, and despite the fact that many of its variants were mere "lash-ups", the performance of the aircraft was never so degraded as to become seriously vulnerable – as the Dornier and Heinkel bombers were.

The most important early model was the Ju 88A, of which some 7000 or more were delivered in variants up to the Ju 88A-17 with steadily uprated engines, enhanced defensive armament and improved offensive capability. The final total of 15,000 Ju 88s of all models gives an idea of the significance of this aircraft, which as well as its bombing role was also developed to serve as a night-fighter, close-support and big-gun anti-armour machine, and missile-carrying reconnaissance platform.

MESSERSCHMITT Bf 109

The Bf 109 was the standard Luftwaffe fighter of the war, with more than 30,500 examples built before and during it. Willy Messerschmitt began work on this classic machine in 1935, in response to Germany's requirement for its first "modern" monoplane fighter (see Heinkel He 112). It was revealed in September 1935, when the first of 13 prototypes flew. The Bf 109B entered service in April 1937 and was followed by the Bf 109C with extra guns. Both saw service in the Spanish Civil War. They were followed by the Bf 109D and the Bf 109E ("Emil"), which entered service at the end of 1938 and was Germany's standard single-seat fighter at the start of World War II – instrumental in Luftwaffe successes over Poland, Scandinavia and the Low Countries.

Only when it took part in the Battle of Britain were its limitations realized. Predictably, the Bf 109 was developed into many variants – when standardization would have benefited the war effort. Engines, armament, nose profiles, cockpit hoods, modified flying services and the like were all refined in attempts to maintain combat proficiency. The most numerous variant (23,500) was the Bf 109G, but few of those who flew it would dispute that improvements in the type's speed and firepower – gained by the introduction of the more powerful DB 605 engine – resulted in poorer overall handling qualities.

SPECIFICATIONS

MESSERSCHMITT Bf 109

Manufacturer:
Messerschmitt A.G

Type:
Fighter, Fighter-Bomber

Length:
8.85m (29ft 0.5in)

Span:
9.92m (32ft 6.5in)

Height:
2.50m (8ft 2.5in)

Maximum speed:
621km/h (386mph)

Service ceiling:
11,550m (37,890ft)

Range:
1000km (621 miles)

Crew:
One

Powerplant:
1 x DB 605

Armament:
1 x cannon, 2 x MG

Bomb load:
250kg (551lb)

First flight:
Late 1935

Initial climb:
950m (3116ft) per min

Weight (empty):
2673kg (5893lb)

Weight (loaded):
3400kg (7496lb)

MESSERSCHMITT Bf 110

SPECIFICATIONS

MESSERSCHMITT Bf 110

Manufacturer: **Messerschmitt A.G**	Crew: **2/3**
Type: **Heavy Fighter**	Powerplant: **2 x DB 601A-1**
Length: **12.10m (39ft 8.33in)**	Armament: **1 x cannon, 5 x MG**
Span: **16.20m (53ft 1.8in)**	Bomb load: **Not Available**
Height: **4.13m (13ft 6.5in)**	First flight: **2 May 1936**
Maximum speed: **560km/h (248mph)**	Initial climb: **585m (1755ft) per min**
Service ceiling: **10,000m (32,810ft)6**	Weight (empty): **5150kg (11,354lb)**
Range: **1095km (680 miles)**	Weight (loaded): **6750kg (14,881lb)**

During the 1930s air strategists believed twin-engine "heavy fighters" to be essential to offensive air operations. As was happening elsewhere at the same time, in 1934 the Reichsluftfahrtministerium issued a requirement for a machine capable of tackling aircraft, including single-seat fighters, sent up to intercept the bombers; it was to make up in firepower what it lacked in manoeuvrability and was dubbed *Zerstörer* (destroyer). Messerschmitt's prototype Bf 110V1 first flew in May 1936 and the production Bf 110 entered service as the Bf 110B with two 700hp (522kW) Junkers Jumo 210 engines. Only 45 were built before the advent of the Bf 110C with two Daimler-Benz DB 601 engines, which had seven sub-variants, and the Bf 110D, built in three.

Pitched against smaller, lighter fighter aircraft during the Battle of Britain, the Bf 110 proved vulnerable and from autumn 1940 production of the indifferent Bf 110C/D was scaled down. In spring 1941 two new variants, the -E (light bomber) and -F, appeared. The Bf 110F was introduced to take advantage of the powerful new DB 601F engine, and as the F-4 night-fighter got early Lichtenstein radar equipment. With later night versions -G and -H, in 1944 the Bf 110 represented 60 per cent of the strength of the Luftwaffe night-fighter units. By March 1945 a total of 6050 Bf 110s had been built.

MESSERSCHMITT 323

Originally planned as a heavy tank and troop transport glider, and first flown on 25 February 1941, the Me 321 V1 prototype had a single-crew member and a substantial cargo hold that could accommodate some 200 troops or 20,000kg (44,092lb) of freight. The Me 321A-1 entered service in late in 1941, followed by the Me 321B-1 with a crew of three and two defensive machine-guns. Luftwaffe transport pilots found that the Me 321 handled adequately in the air, but lacked a suitably powerful tug (even the extraordinary five-engined Heinkel He 111Z proved inadequate). This led to further development as the Me 323 with multi-wheel landing gear, structural strengthening and six Gnome-Rhòne radial engines from captured French stocks.

The initial production variant was the Me 323D-1 with the ability to carry a payload of 9750kg (21,495lb), including 120 troops or 60 litters, over a range of 1000km (621 miles). Deliveries began in August 1942, and in November of the same year the Me 323Ds were put to work supplying Rommel's beleaguered Afrika Korps across the Mediterranean. The lumbering giant proved easy pickings for Allied pilots and heavy losses were suffered. Later models included the Me 323E, with stronger structure, greater fuel capacity and heavier defensive armament.

SPECIFICATIONS

MESSERSCHMITT 323

Manufacturer: **Messerschmitt A.G**	*Crew:* **10/11**
Type: **Heavy Transport**	*Powerplant:* **6 x Gnome-Rhòne radials**
Length: **28.5m (93ft 6in)**	*Armament:* **1 x 20mm; 5 x MG**
Span: **55m (180ft 5.33in)**	*Bomb load:* **None**
Height: **9.6m (31ft 6in)**	*First flight:* **1942**
Maximum speed: **253km/h (157mph)**	*Initial climb:* **N/A**
Service ceiling: **4500m (14,760ft)**	*Weight (empty):* **29,600kg (65,256lb)**
Range: **1300km (808 miles)**	*Weight (loaded):* **45,000kg (99,206lb)**

MESSERSCHMITT
Me 410

SPECIFICATIONS

MESSERSCHMITT Me 410

Manufacturer:
Messerschmitt A.G

Crew:
Two

Type:
Heavy Fighter

Powerplant:
2 x DB 603A

Length:
12.48m (40ft 11.5in)

Armament:
4 x cannon, 4 x MG

Span:
16.35m (53ft 7.75in)

Bomb load:
Not Available

Height:
4.28m (14ft 0.5in)

First flight:
1942

Maximum speed:
624km/h (388mph)

Initial climb:
628m (2060ft) per min

Service ceiling:
10,000m (32,810ft)

Weight (empty):
7518kg (16,574lb)

Range:
1670km (1050 miles)

Weight (loaded):
10,650kg (23,483lb)

In 1937 Messerschmitt began developing the Bf 210, planned as a more versatile successor to the Bf 110. In June 1939 an order for 1000 aircraft was placed "off the drawing board", but after prototype Me 210V1 had revealed flight instability and landing gear problems, progress foundered. Production aircraft were delivered from late 1941 but in service it was a complete flop and production ended after 352 machines. The failure of the Me 210 nearly cost Willy Messerschmitt his job. Key aspects of the design were changed to produce the Me 410, which proved to be an altogether more capable as well as more successful warplane. The Me 210's failings had in fact been solved just before its cancellation, and it was from this type that the Me 410 was evolved, with basically the same revised aerodynamic and structural features in combination with modified outer wing panels and the different powerplant of two Daimler-Benz DB 603A inverted-Vee piston engines. The Me 410 first flew in prototype form in autumn 1942, and there followed 1137 production aircraft in variants such as the Me 410A (three major variants) and the Me 410B. Five major variants of the 410B were produced with the DB 603G engines. The B-5 anti-shipping torpedo bomber, the B-7 day reconnaissance and B-8 night reconnaissance aircraft were still in the experimental stage at the war's end.

AVRO ANSON

During a production run that lasted from 1934 to 1952, this ubiquitous aircraft was built in larger numbers than any other British aeroplane except the Hawker Hurricane and Supermarine Spitfire. The Anson was initially conceived as a light transport for Imperial Airways and entered service with the carrier as the Avro 652 in March 1936. The design was also adapted to 652A standard with a dorsal turret and square rather then round windows, to meet an Air Ministry specification issued in May 1934 that called for a twin-engined landplane to be used in the coastal reconnaissance role.

The prototype first flew in March 1935, and the type was ordered into production as the Anson Mk I (later Anson GR.Mk I) with other minor modifications to the tail unit, and powered by 250kW (335hp) Armstrong Siddeley Cheetah IX radial seven-cylinder, single-row radial engines (later aircraft received uprated 295kW/-395hp Cheetah XIX engines).

The first of these aircraft flew in December 1935, and the type entered service in March of the following year at the start of a programme that saw the delivery of 6915 aircraft. As well as its coastal reconnaissance role, the Anson was also adapted for use as an advanced flying, navigation and gunnery trainer and also for use as a communications aircraft.

SPECIFICATIONS

AVRO ANSON

Manufacturer: **A.V. Roe & Co., Ltd.**	Crew: **3/4**
Type: **Coastal Reconnaissance**	Powerplant: **2 x Cheetah IX**
Length: **12.88m (42ft 3in)**	Armament: **4 x 0.303in MG**
Span: **17.22m (56ft 6in))**	Bomb load: **227kg (500lb)**
Height: **3.99m (13ft 1in)**	First flight: **March 1935**
Maximum speed: **303km/h (188mph)**	Initial climb: **293m (960ft) per min**
Service ceiling: **5790m (19,000ft)**	Weight (empty): **2438kg (5375lb)**
Range: **1271 km (790km)**	Weight (loaded): **4218kg (9300lb)**

AVRO LANCASTER

SPECIFICATIONS

AVRO LANCASTER

Manufacturer:
A.V. Roe & Co., Ltd.

Crew:
Seven

Type:
Heavy Bomber

Powerplant:
4 x RR Merlin XX

Length:
21.18m (69ft 6in)

Armament:
9 x 0.303in MG

Span:
31.09m (102ft 0in)

Bomb load:
8165kg (18,000lb)

Height:
6.25m (20ft 6in)

First flight:
9 January 1941

Maximum speed:
462km/h (287mph)

Initial climb:
76m (250ft) per min

Service ceiling:
5790m (19,000ft)

Weight (empty):
16,783kg (37,000lb)

Range:
2784km (1730 miles)

Weight (loaded):
29,484kg (65,000lb)

The most successful heavy night bomber used by the Royal Air Force in World War II, the Lancaster was a development of the underpowered Manchester with the revised powerplant of four Rolls-Royce (RR) Merlin 12-cylinder Vee engines. The Lancaster first flew on 9 January 1941 and entered service from the beginning of 1942. It soon developed a reputation as a sturdy aeroplane that handled well in the air, possessed moderately good performance, and had good defensive and offensive firepower. The fact that the design was "right" from the beginning is reflected by the very small number of changes made during the course of a long production run that covered 10 variants.

The demand for Merlin engines soon outgrew Rolls-Royce's production capacity, resulting in the decision to use the American licence-built version, namely the Packard V-1650 in its Merlin 28, 38 or 224 forms. Installed in the Lancaster Mk I, the aeroplane was known as the Lancaster Mk III (later B.Mk III and finally B.Mk 3) and was also produced in Canada by Victory Aircraft Ltd. of Toronto. Special versions were built for the carrying of the bouncing bombs used on the famous raids against the Ruhr Dams and for dropping deep-penetration-type bombs (5443kg/12,000lb "Tallboy" and 9979kg/22,000lb "Grand Slam".)

AVRO LINCOLN

The third outgrowth of the Manchester was the Type 694 Lincoln, designed to British Air Ministry Specification B14/43 as the replacement for the Lancaster. Originally known as the Lancaster IV, and resembling its more famous brother, the new aircraft was intended to fly farther and higher, gaining a new wing, longer fuselage, heavier armament and stronger landing gear. H2S radar was fitted as standard.

The first unarmed prototype flew in June 1944, later gaining a Martin dorsal turret. The second prototype flew in November 1944 with a Bristol dorsal turret, this being the definitive form for production aircraft. The first production machines were delivered in February 1945 but although plans for mass production by three manufacturers had been laid, production was scaled down after VE Day in May 1945 and totalled only 72 Mk Is and 465 Mk IIs. Bomber Command squadrons began to take delivery in August, some months later than originally scheduled and too late for the Lincoln to see operational service in World War II.

The Lincoln remained in Royal Air Force service until replaced by the Canberra in the early 1950s. This great family of Avro aircraft found its ultimate realization in the Shackleton, which served with the Royal Air Force until the mid-1980s.

SPECIFICATIONS

AVRO LINCOLN

Manufacturer: **A.V. Roe & Co. Ltd.**	Crew: **Seven**
Type: **Heavy Bomber**	Powerplant: **4 x RR Merlin 85**
Length: **23.86m (78ft 3.5in)**	Armament: **6 x 0.50in MG**
Span: **36.58m (120ft)**	Bomb load: **6350kg (14,000lb)**
Height: **5.27m (17ft 3.5in)**	First flight: **9 June 1944**
Maximum speed: **475km/h (295mph)**	Initial climb: **Not Available**
Service ceiling: **9295m (30,500ft)**	Weight (empty): **19,686kg (43,400lb)**
Range: **2366km (1470 miles)**	Weight (loaded): **34,019kg (75,000lb)**

AVRO MANCHESTER

SPECIFICATIONS

AVRO MANCHESTER

Manufacturer: **A.V. Roe & Co. Ltd.**	Crew: **Seven**
Type: **Medium Bomber**	Powerplant: **2 x RR Vulture X-type**
Length: **21.14m (69ft 4.25in)**	Armament: **8 x 0.303in MG**
Span: **27.46m (90ft 1in)**	Bomb load: **4695kg (10,350lb)**
Height: **5.94m (19ft 6in)**	First flight: **25 July 1939**
Maximum speed: **426km/h (265mph)**	Initial climb: **Not Available**
Service ceiling: **5850m (19,200ft)**	Weight (empty): **13,350kg (29,432lb)**
Range: **2623km (1630 miles)**	Weight (loaded): **25,402kg (56,000lb)**

During the inter-war period the Air Ministry concentrated much of its resources on building up a fleet of bombers, in line with the doctrine of the day on future offensive air operations. In 1936 the ministry issued a requirement that elicited responses from both Avro and Handley Page. Both companies received prototype orders although the Handley Page H.P 56 did not progress beyond the drawing board (the company preferring instead to focus on development of the Halifax), thus allowing a clear field for the Avro design.

The first of two Manchester prototypes flew in July 1939, after an initial order for 200 aircraft had been placed to the revised 19/37 Specification. Following flight trials the wing span was increased by 3m (10ft) and a central fin was added. The Manchester Mk I became operational in November 1940 with No 207 Squadron at Waddington, and these 20 aircraft were followed by 180 examples of the Manchester Mk IA with larger endplate vertical surfaces on the tail, allowing the removal of the Mk I's centreline surface. In service the Manchester was a failure; despite having an ideal airframe, the twin Vulture did not provide sufficient power and was wholly unreliable. By the time that the Manchester was retired in June 1942, 40 per cent of the 202 aircraft had been lost on operations and another 25 per cent had crashed.

AVRO YORK

During the war, RAF Transport Command was supplied with American aircraft, under a contract that freed the British aircraft industry to concentrate on fighter and bomber production. Avro designers under Roy Chadwick nevertheless went ahead with the design of a four-engine long-range passenger and cargo transport aircraft, a process which they completed in February 1942. The new aircraft mated the wings, tail assembly, engines and landing gear with a new fuselage of roughly rectangular section fitted with large hatches to enable bulky items to be loaded. After the first flight in July 1942, an official order was placed for four aircraft. The third aircraft against this order gained a third fin to compensate for the additional side area of the forward fuselage and in this form was delivered to the RAF as the York I from March 1943.

This was the first of a number of aircraft that were fitted out for VIP transport duties and in the ensuing months carried such dignitaries as King George VI and Prime Minister Winston Churchill across the globe. With Avro fully occupied with the production of Lancaster bombers, only a small number of Yorks were built before 1944, when the aircraft was put into mass production. Some 257 were built in all and eventually 10 RAF squadrons were equipped with the type.

SPECIFICATIONS

AVRO YORK

Manufacturer: **A.V. Roe & Co. Ltd.**	Crew: **Four**
Type: **Long-Range Transport**	Powerplant: **4 x RR Merlin XX**
Length: **23.93m (78ft 6in)**	Armament: **None**
Span: **31.09m (102ft 6in)**	Bomb load: **None**
Height: **5.44m (17ft 10in)**	First flight: **5 July 1942**
Maximum speed: **480km/h (298mph)**	Initial climb: **Not Available**
Service ceiling: **7010m (23,000ft)**	Weight (empty): **19,069kg (42,040lb)**
Range: **4345km (2700 miles)**	Weight (loaded): **31,115kg (68,597lb)**

BLACKBURN SKUA

SPECIFICATIONS

BLACKBURN SKUA

Manufacturer: Blackburn Aircraft, Ltd	**Crew:** Two
Type: Carrier-Borne Fighter	**Powerplant:** 1 x Bristol Perseus XII
Length: 10.85m (35ft 7in)	**Armament:** 4 x 0.303in MG
Span: 14.07m (46ft 2in)	**Bomb load:** 227kg (500lb)
Height: 3.81m (12ft 6in)	**First flight:** 9 February 1937
Maximum speed: 362km/h (225mph)	**Initial climb:** 482m (1580ft) per min
Service ceiling: 6160m (20,200ft)	**Weight (empty):** 2490kg (5490lb)
Range: 1223km (760 miles)	**Weight (loaded):** 3732kg (8228lb)

In 1937 the Blackburn Company received a contract for the production of the Skua fighter dive-bomber. In 1934 the Air Ministry had somewhat belatedly recognised the very real shortage of such aircraft within the navy, and issued specification O.27/34 that also brought submissions from Avro, Boulton Paul, Hawker and Vickers. Blackburn's design was selected and two of the Blackburn aircraft were built for evaluation.

The first prototype flew in February 1937, by which time orders for 190 had already been placed. The Skua represented a significant break from the Royal Navy's traditional carrier-borne biplanes; it was the UK's first naval dive-bomber, and the country's first deck-landing aircraft to have flaps, retractable landing gear and a variable pitch propeller. Deliveries of the first production aircraft were made in October 1938 and at the outbreak of war there were squadrons of them embarked on HMS *Ark Royal* and HMS *Furious*. Much was expected of the Skua when war broke out.

In service the aircraft performed creditably in the dive-bombing role during the battle for Norway in 1940, but it was hampered by very limited range and served only until 1941, after which they were progressively replaced by Fairey Fulmars. The survivors were employed for target-towing and for training.

BOULTON PAUL DEFIANT

By 1933 the enclosed gun turret, manually worked or power-driven, was being studied intensely. The two main attractions were reduced pilot workload and the turret's significantly greater field of fire. First seen on the Hawker Demon in 1936 and on a whole class of French aircraft that were festooned with turrets, Boulton Paul's Defiant was the British design. It was a bold attempt to combine the performance of the new monoplanes with a powered turret carrying four Browning machine guns. The gunner had a control column which moved left/right for rotation, fore/aft for depression and elevation and with a safety/firing button on top. The prototype flew in August 1937 and trials confirmed that it was not unpleasant to fly, and not terribly degraded in performance by carrying a crew of two and a heavy turret. It entered service in December 1939 and achieved some success over France in May 1940. German pilots, though, soon learned to use the greater agility of their lighter fighters to engage the Defiant head-on or from below, where the guns could not be trained, and losses soared. The Defiant was subsequently utilized as a night-fighter and finally for target-towing duties. Production was 723 Mk I and NF.Mk I machines, 210 Mk II and NF.Mk II aircraft with the Merlin XX engine, and 140 TT.Mk I machines ordered as Mk II fighters.

SPECIFICATIONS

BOULTON PAUL DEFIANT

Manufacturer: **Boulton Paul Aircraft**	Crew: **Two**
Type: **(Defiant Mk I) Fighter**	Powerplant: **1 x RR Merlin III**
Length: **10.77m (35ft 4in)**	Armament: **4 x 0.303in MG**
Span: **11.99m (39ft 4in)**	Bomb load: **None**
Height: **4.39m (14ft 5in)**	First flight: **11 August 1937**
Maximum speed: **489km/h (304mph)**	Initial climb: **565m (1852ft) per min**
Service ceiling: **9250m (30,350ft)**	Weight (empty): **2757kg (6078lb)**
Range: **748km (465 miles)**	Weight (loaded): **3788kg (8350lb)**

BRISTOL BEAUFIGHTER

SPECIFICATIONS

BRISTOL BEAUFIGHTER

Manufacturer:
Bristol Aeroplane Co.

Crew:
Two

Type:
Heavy/Night-Fighter

Powerplant:
2 x Bristol Hercules VI

Length:
12.70m (41ft 8in)

Armament:
4 x cannon, 6 x MG

Span:
17.63m (57ft 10in)

Bomb load:
None

Height:
4.82m (15ft 10in)

First flight:
17 July 1939

Maximum speed:
536km/h (333mph)

Initial climb:
564m (1850ft) per min

Service ceiling:
8077m (26,500ft)

Weight (empty):
6622kg (14,600lb)

Range:
2478km (1540 miles)

Weight (loaded):
9798kg (21,600lb)

During the years 1935–39 the most glaring gaps in the RAF's armoury were the lack of any long-range fighter, any cannon-armed fighter and any fighter capable of effective bomber escort and night-fighting. These deficiencies were sorely exposed in the first years of the war, until aircraft capable of performing adequately in these roles became available. The Beaufighter was one such aircraft.

Despite the lack of an official requirement for such an aircraft, Bristol designed it as a private venture. They created a heavy fighter derivative of the Beaufort torpedo bomber, incorporating some 75 per cent of its airframe components and when Bristol's chief engineer proposed it to the Air Ministry it was received with enthusiasm. First flown in July 1939 as a heavy fighter, the aircraft entered service in July 1940 with a smaller fuselage and an uprated powerplant, and as the need for effective night-fighters became acute the radar-equipped Mk IF was introduced. The 397 Mk IC coastal fighters were fitted with Hercules engines and later complemented by 597 Mk IIF night-fighters with 954kW (1280hp) Rolls-Royce Merlin XX Vee engines. Subsequent versions were equipped with rockets and torpedoes for anti-shipping work, and as better radar became available the night fighter "Beau" gained a thimble nose fairing.

BRISTOL BLENHEIM

The Blenheim was a militarized version of the Type 142 high-speed light transport Bristol originally designed for Lord Rothermere. Its derivative entered service as a light bomber in 1939, when it was hoped that it would both prove operationally capable within the RAF and help to create a pool of skilled aircrews pending the development of high-performance types.

Despite extensive service it never proved truly effective; the first variant was the Blenheim Mk I, some of which were converted to Blenheim Mk IF night-fighter standard with a ventral pack of four 0.303in machine guns and radar. The Mk IV was designed to overcome the deficiencies of the Mk I, and had an uprated powerplant, significantly increased fuel capacity and a longer forward fuselage to accommodate a navigator's station. The Mk IV bomber equipped a total of 45 squadrons in the UK, Middle East and Far East, and numbers of the aircraft were later converted to Mk IVF night-fighter standard with a ventral gun pack and radar. The Mk V was a final attempt to wring improved performance out of the airframe and was basically the Mk IV with a revised forward fuselage with four fixed forward-firing machine guns, an improved windscreen, more armour, a dorsal turret with a gyro sight, and engines optimized for medium-altitude operations.

SPECIFICATIONS

BRISTOL BLENHEIM

Manufacturer: **Bristol Aeroplane Co.**	Crew: **Three**
Type: **Light Bomber**	Powerplant: **2 x Bristol Mercury VIII**
Length: **12.12m (39ft 9in)**	Armament: **2 x 0.303in MG**
Span: **17.17m (56ft 4in)**	Bomb load: **454kg (1000lb)**
Height: **3.00m (9ft 10in)**	First flight: **25 June 1936**
Maximum speed: **459km/h (285mph)**	Initial climb: **457m (1499ft) per min**
Service ceiling: **Not Given**	Weight (empty): **4013kg (8839lb)**
Range: **1810km(1125 miles)**	Weight (loaded): **5947kg (13,100lb)**

DE HAVILLAND MOSQUITO

SPECIFICATIONS

DE HAVILLAND MOSQUITO

Manufacturer: **De Havilland Aircraft Co.**	Crew: **Two**
Type: **Light Bomber**	Powerplant: **2 x RR Merlin**
Length: **13.56m (44ft 6in)**	Armament: **None**
Span: **16.51m (54ft 2in)**	Bomb load: **1814kg (4000lb)**
Height: **4.65m (15ft 3in)**	First flight: **25 November 1940**
Maximum speed: **668km/h (415mph)**	Initial climb: **609m (1999ft) per min**
Service ceiling: **11,280m (37,000ft)**	Weight (empty): **7031kg (15,500lb)**
Range: **2888km (1795 miles)**	Weight (loaded): **11,766kg (25,917lb)**

Undeniably one of the most important aircraft of the war, and rivalled only by the Junkers Ju 88 in terms of its versatility, the Mosquito was developed from October 1938 as a private venture to provide the Royal Air Force with a high-speed unarmed day bomber, with the added attraction of wooden construction to ease the burden on British supplies of aircraft grade metals.

The Air Ministry initially showed no interest. In 1940, with extreme reluctance, it allowed the company to proceed. Built largely of a ply/balsa/ply sandwich material, the Mosquito Mk I prototype first flew in November 1940 and paved the way for a mass of variants totalling some 7781 aircraft. The Mosquito's versatility and high performance meant that the type was developed in forms other than the originally planned bomber. There were nine night-fighter versions, the first of which became operational as the Mosquito NF.Mk II from May 1942, armed with four 20mm cannon and four 0.303in machine guns as well as AI.Mk IV radar.

There were also many unarmed photo-reconnaissance and bomber variants, with progressively improved armament, engines, fuel and avionics. The heavily armed FB.XVIII variant, dubbed the "Tsetse Fly", had a 57mm Molins gun plus four 0.303in Brownings and eight rockets or bombs.

FAIREY ALBACORE

Although designed to supersede the Fairey Swordfish as the primary torpedo bomber of the Fleet Air Arm, the Albacore was in fact only able to complement the Swordfish in this role; in many respects the older aircraft was able to outperform the Albacore as well as outlive it by more than one year. Schemed to Specification S.41/36, the Albacore was ordered off the drawing board in May 1937, the Air Ministry ordering two prototypes and 98 production aircraft. It was in effect a modernized and technically somewhat improved development of the Swordfish with enclosed accommodation, a higher-rated engine, hydraulically operated flaps and a number of aerodynamic revisions designed to reduce drag.

The first of two Albacore prototypes made its maiden flight in December 1938; and one was later tested with floats, but the results did not justify any further development of a floatplane. The first of 798 Albacore Mk I production aircraft entered service in March 1940, initially as a land-based type and only from 1941 on board aircraft carriers. The aircraft was notably involved in the Battle of Cape Matapan in March 1941 and by mid-1942 some 15 Fleet Air Arm squadrons were equipped with the type, yet it spawned no improved models, and was withdrawn from first-line service in 1944.

SPECIFICATIONS

FAIREY ALBACORE

Manufacturer: Fairey Aviation Co.	**Crew:** Three
Type: Torpedo Bomber	**Powerplant:** 1 x Bristol Taurus XII
Length: 12.18m (39ft 11.75in)	**Armament:** 3 x 0.303in MG
Span: 15.23m (49ft 11.75in)	**Bomb or torpedo load:** 907kg (2000lb)
Height: 3.81m (12ft 6in)	**First flight:** 12 December 1938
Maximum speed: 57km/h (161mph)	**Initial climb:** 228m (750ft) per min
Service ceiling: 6310m (20,700ft)	**Weight (empty):** 3269kg (7200lb)
Range: 1497km (930 miles)	**Weight (loaded):** 5670kg (12,500lb)

FAIREY BARRACUDA

SPECIFICATIONS

FAIREY BARRACUDA

Manufacturer: **Fairey Aviation Co.**	Crew: **Three**
Type: **Naval Torpedo Bomber**	Powerplant: **1 x RR Merlin 32**
Length: **12.12m (39ft 9in)**	Armament: **2 x 0.303in MG**
Span: **15m (49ft 2in)**	Bomb load: **735kg (1617lb)**
Height: **4.6m (15ft 1in)**	First flight: **7 December 1940**
Maximum speed: **367km/h (228mph)**	Initial climb: **290m (950ft) per min**
Service ceiling: **5060m (16,600ft)**	Weight (empty): **4241kg (9350lb)**
Range: **1101km (684 miles)**	Weight (loaded): **6396kg (14,100lb)**

To replace the Albacore in service, Specification S.24/37 was drawn up and had it not been so severely delayed the resultant Barracuda may have played a greater part in World War II. The first delay, from 1938 to 1940, was due to the abandonment of the proposed Rolls-Royce Exe engine, and the low-rated Merlin was only marginally powerful enough for an aircraft as big and heavy as the Barracuda.

The pressure of other programmes held back production for two years, but in May 1943 No 827 Sqn of the Fleet Air Arm was at last fully equipped with Barracudas. In April of the following year a force of 42 aircraft, flying off the carriers HMS *Victorious* and HMS *Furious*, scored 15 direct hits on the German battleship *Tirpitz* as it lay in Kaafjord, for the loss of only two aircraft.

The Mk II version had a more powerful engine and a four-blade propeller, and it was later equipped with ASV.IIN radar. For the Mk III version ASV.10 was fitted in an underfuselage radome. In 1945 the powerful Mk V version, called the TF.5, was produced, with redesigned structure and accommodation – but only 30 of these were built, and the variant never entered front-line service, although the last Barracudas were not retired until 1953.

FAIREY BATTLE

At the outbreak of World War II the Fairey Battle was the RAF's most numerous day bomber, yet it suffered appalling losses at the hands of German fighters because it was completely unable to defend itself from them. Its evolution began in 1932; at this time the Battle represented a major advance over the Hawker Hart and Hind light bomber biplanes that it was designed to replace in Royal Air Force service.

The Battle was a cantilever, stressed-skin monoplane which epitomized modern design and carried twice the bomb load for twice the distance at 50 per cent higher speeds. It was the first aircraft to go into production with the new Rolls Royce Merlin engine, but nonetheless was technically and tactically obsolescent by the time it entered service in March 1937, as a result of the rapid pace of aeronautical development during the approach to World War II.

Production of the Battle light bomber totalled 1818 from two British manufacturers for RAF service (subsequently redesignated as the Battle Mks I to V depending on the mark of engine installed) and 18 Belgian-built aircraft for Belgian service. The type was relegated to second-line service in 1940 as the Battle (T) trainer and Battle (TT) target-tug, of which 100 and 266 respectively were built to supplement conversions.

SPECIFICATIONS

FAIREY BATTLE

Manufacturer: **Fairey Aviation Co.**	Crew: **2/3**
Type: **Light Day Bomber**	Powerplant: **1 x RR Merlin II**
Length: **12.93m (42ft 5in)**	Armament: **1 x 0.303in MG**
Span: **16.45m (54ft)**	Bomb load: **680kg (1500lb)**
Height: **4.57m (15ft)**	First flight: **10 March 1936**
Maximum speed: **406km/h (252mph)**	Initial climb: **280m (920ft) per min**
Service ceiling: **7925m (26,000ft)**	Weight (empty): **3361kg (7410lb)**
Range: **1931km (1200 miles)**	Weight (loaded): **5307kg (11,700lb)**

FAIREY SWORDFISH

SPECIFICATIONS

FAIREY SWORDFISH

Manufacturer: **Fairey Aviation Co.**	Crew: **Three**
Type: **Torpedo Bomber Biplane**	Powerplant: **1 x Bristol Pegasus III**
Length: **11.12m (36ft 4in)**	Armament: **2 x 0.303in MG**
Span: **13.92m (45ft 6in)**	Bomb load: **731kg (1610lb) torpedo**
Height: **3.93m (12ft 10in)**	First flight: **17 April 1934**
Maximum speed: **222km/h (138mph)**	Initial climb: **372m (1220ft) per min**
Service ceiling: **3260m (10,700ft)**	Weight (empty): **2359kg (5200lb)**
Range: **885km (550 miles)**	Weight (loaded): **4196kg (9250lb)**

Despite looking archaic even when new, when tested in combat some ten years after it first appeared on the Fairey drawing board the Swordfish proved to be superbly effective. In September 1930 the Air Ministry issued a specification calling for a torpedo-carrying fleet spotter. In response Fairey built the TSR 1, powered by a 474kW (635hp) Bristol Pegasus radial engine, and first flew it in March 1933. After some revisions to cure stability problems it was ordered into production as the Swordfish Mk I in 1935. Later versions were the Mk II, with a strengthened lower wing skinned on its lower surfaces with metal rather than the fabric of the Mk I to permit the carriage and firing of up to eight 76mm (3in) air-to-surface rockets, and the Mk III, a development of the Mk II with improved anti-submarine capability bestowed by the addition of ASV.Mk X air-to-surface search radar with its antenna in a large radome between the main landing gear legs. In service the Swordfish gained a reputation for ruggedness, reliability, versatility in terms of weapons and equipment, and such viceless handling that it could be flown in most weather conditions from bases ranging in size from the largest fleet carriers to the smallest of escort carriers. Its most famous hour was the torpedo attack on the Italian fleet at Taranto in November 1940, a truly decisive action.

GLOSTER SEA GLADIATOR

Although designed to a specification written in 1930, when biplane fighters were already entering their final phase of development, the Gladiator was not ordered into production for nearly five years, by which time war in Europe was looming and the pace of aircraft development had consigned the fabric-covered biplane to the history books. However, despite being something of an anachronism, the Gladiator was undoubtedly the finest British biplane fighter, being a development of the Gauntlet with improved features such as an enclosed cockpit, trailing-edge flaps and cantilever main landing gear legs. The prototype flew in September 1934, and the first of 378 Gladiator Mk I fighters entered service in 1937 pending the large-scale advent of more advanced monoplane fighters.

The Gladiator Mk I was supplemented by the Gladiator Mk II, of which 311 were delivered with the Mercury VIIIA or VIIIAS engine and desert filters, auto-mixture control and electric starting from an internal battery. Some 38 of the aircraft were converted to Interim Sea Gladiator standard, paving the way for the carrier-borne Sea Gladiator of which 60 were completed. The Gladiator saw first-line service in the northern European and Mediterranean theatres to 1940 and the middle of 1941, and numbers of the aircraft were also exported.

SPECIFICATIONS

GLOSTER SEA GLADIATOR

Manufacturer: **Gloster Aircraft Co.**	Crew: **One**
Type: **Fighter Biplane**	Powerplant: **1 x Bristol Mercury IX**
Length: **8.36m (27ft 5in)**	Armament: **2 x 0.303in MG**
Span: **9.83m (32ft 3in)**	Bomb load: **None**
Height: **3.53m (11ft 7in)**	First flight: **September 1934**
Maximum speed: **414km/h (257mph)**	Initial climb: **700m (2300ft) per min**
Service ceiling: **10,120m (33,500ft)**	Weight (empty): **1562kg (3444lb)**
Range: **708km (440 miles)**	Weight (loaded): **2206kg (4864lb)**

GLOSTER METEOR

SPECIFICATIONS

GLOSTER METEOR

Manufacturer: **Gloster Aircraft Co.**	Crew: **One**
Type: **Single-Seat Fighter**	Powerplant: **2 x RR Derwent turbojet**
Length: **13.58m (44ft 7in)**	Armament: **4 x 20mm cannon**
Span: **11.32m (37ft 2in)**	Bomb load: **None**
Height: **3.96m (13ft)**	First flight: **5 March 1943**
Maximum speed: **962km/h (598mph)**	Initial climb: **2200m (7216ft) per min**
Service ceiling: **13,106m (43,000ft)**	Weight (empty): **4820kg (10,626lb)**
Range: **1580km (980 miles)**	Weight (loaded): **8664kg (19,100lb)**

Britain's first operational jet combat aircraft, and the only such Allied aircraft to see service during World War II, the Gloster Meteor was designed by George Carter to meet a specification laid down in 1940. Initially, it was to have been called the Thunderbolt, but when this name was given to the P-47 the Gloster twin-jet became the Meteor. As with the Me 262 progress was hampered by delays in developing engines that could deliver sufficient power, this was exacerbated in the case of the Meteor by problems with the nosewheel ailerons and tail and its relatively large size. Numerous different installations were trialled for the Meteor, including the Rolls-Royce W.2B, the de Havilland-developed Halford H.1 and the Metrovick F.2.

The first 20 production aircraft were delivered in July 1944 with Rolls-Royce Welland engines, and were immediately pressed into service chasing flying bombs over southern England. The first major production version was the F.3, which had Derwent turbojet engines, extra tankage and a sliding canopy; the aircraft was subsequently developed in a number of forms with more powerful engines as a fighter, reconnaissance platform, night-fighter and trainer. Production of the aircraft ended in May 1954 and amounted to 3947 aircraft, including 480 that were licence-built.

HANDLEY PAGE HALIFAX

Designed to the same P.13/36 Specification as the Lancaster, the Halifax never achieved the fame of the Avro aircraft despite making almost as great a contribution to the Allied effort and in a greater diversity of roles, also undertaking maritime reconnaissance, transport and airborne forces work. The two prototypes, of which the first flew in October 1939, were followed by the Halifax Mk I that entered service in November 1940 with 954kW (1280hp) Rolls-Royce Merlin X Vee engines, and the Halifax Mk II with 1036kW (1390hp) Merlin XX or XXII engines. The Halifax Mk III saw a switch to Bristol Hercules radial engines; 2091 aircraft were made by five manufacturers. The Mk V, of which 904 were completed by two manufacturers in three sub-series, was an improved Mk II and was delivered in both bomber and maritime reconnaissance forms. Some early Halifax aircraft were converted for the glider-towing role, as troop transports with fuselage accommodation for up to 24 men, or else for the clandestine insertion of agents and equipment by parachute into enemy territory. No.100 Group of Bomber Command operated Halifax bombers converted for the electronic countermeasures role to degrade the capabilities of the Germans' radar and radio systems as an aid to other more conventional operations. Post-war, many became passenger transports.

SPECIFICATIONS

HANDLEY PAGE HALIFAX

Manufacturer: Handley Page Ltd.	**Crew:** Seven
Type: Heavy Bomber	**Powerplant:** 4 x Bristol Hercules VI
Length: 21.74m (71ft 4in)	**Armament:** 9 x 0.303in MG
Span: 30.07m (98ft 8in)	**Bomb load:** 6577kg (14,500lb)
Height: 6.12m (20ft 1in)	**First flight:** 25 October 1939
Maximum speed: 454km/h (282mph)	**Initial climb:** 229m (750ft) per min
Service ceiling: 7315m (24,000ft)	**Weight (empty):** 19,278kg (42,500lb)
Range: 3194km (1985 miles)	**Weight (loaded):** 29,484kg (65,000lb)

HANDLEY PAGE HAMPDEN

SPECIFICATIONS

HANDLEY PAGE HAMPDEN

Manufacturer:
Handley Page Ltd.

Crew:
Four

Type:
Medium Bomber

Powerplant:
2 x Bristol Pegasus

Length:
16.33m (53ft 7in)

Armament:
6 x 0.303in MG

Span:
21.08 m (69ft 2in)

Bomb load:
1814kg (4000lb)

Height:
4.55m (14ft 11in)

First flight:
21 June 1936

Maximum speed:
426km/h (255mph)

Initial climb:
300m (980ft) per min

Service ceiling:
6920m (22,700ft)

Weight (empty):
5343kg (11,780lb)

Range:
3034km (1885 miles)

Weight (loaded):
10,206kg (22,500lb)

On paper the Hampden was a truly outstanding aircraft, and performed well until pitted against German defences in broad daylight. The prototype first flew in June 1936 and performed impressively. While the new aircraft was almost the equal in range of the Whitley and Wellington with a heavy bomb load, it was faster than either; in fact it was almost as fast as the Blenheim, but carried twice the load. The manufacturers themselves considered it so fast and manoeuvrable that they called it "a fighting bomber" and gave the pilot a fixed gun. Three movable defensive guns were adjudged to give all-round defence without the penalties of heavy turrets. Large orders were placed and deliveries of the Hampden Mk I started in September 1938; by the outbreak of war it was one of the most important medium bombers available to the British. Hampdens took part in the early raids on Kiel and Wilhelmshaven, and although hampered by its narrow fuselage, which prevented crew members from taking over the task of another when injured, it proved in many ways to be a good warplane. Heavy losses during daylight operations meant that the "Flying Suitcase" was taken off to be given heavier armour and armament, and thereafter used at night. As more capable types became available it was used for minelaying and torpedo-bombing over the North Sea.

HAWKER HURRICANE

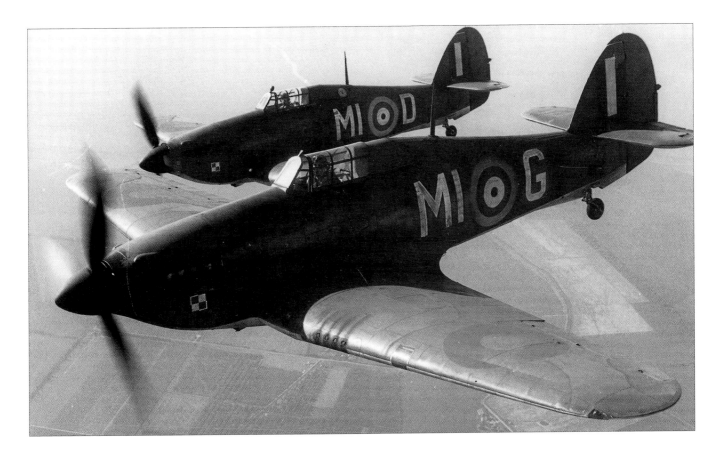

Although the Spitfire is often portrayed as the fighter that "won" the Battle of Britain, it was in fact Sidney Camm's robust and durable Hurricane that destroyed more German aircraft than the rest combined. Well into 1941 it was the RAF's most numerous fighter. Designed as a monoplane version of the earlier Fury, it was not as technically advanced as the Spitfire and had an unstressed, largely fabric, covering. The prototype first flew in November 1935, and the Hurricane Mk I entered service late in 1937 – the RAF's first monoplane fighter. Early aircraft had a two-blade, fixed-pitch propeller that later gave way to a three-blade, constant-speed unit. Some 19 squadrons operated with Mk Is on the outbreak of war and some 32 squadrons were equipped by August 1940. Production totalled about 3650 aircraft. Some 7500 of the improved Mk II fighter-bomber, with an uprated powerplant, heavier armament and enhancements such as metal-skinned wings, three-blade propeller and better protection, were delivered from September 1940 with various configurations. Many aircraft were tropicalized for North African and Far Eastern service with a special chin air filter. The Mk IV was the final British production model and was fitted with uprated engine, additional armour and provision for underwing stores including anti-tank guns. The Sea Hurricane was a naval version.

SPECIFICATIONS

HAWKER HURRICANE

Manufacturer:
Hawker Aircraft Ltd.

Crew:
One

Type:
Single-Seat Fighter

Powerplant:
1 x RR Merlin III

Length:
9.55m (31ft 4in)

Armament:
8 x 0.303in MG

Span:
12.19m (40ft)

Bomb load:
None

Height:
4.07m (13ft 4.5in)

First flight:
6 November 1935

Maximum speed:
521km/h (324mph)

Initial climb:
770m (2520ft) per min

Service ceiling:
10,120m (33,200ft)

Weight (empty):
2308kg (5085lb)

Range:
445 miles (716km)

Weight (loaded):
3024kg (6661lb)

HAWKER TYPHOON

SPECIFICATIONS

HAWKER TYPHOON

Manufacturer: **Hawker Aircraft Ltd.**	Crew: **One**
Type: **Ground-Attack Fighter**	Powerplant: **1 x Napier Sabre**
Length: **9.73m (31ft 11in)**	Armament: **4 x 20mm cannon**
Span: **12.67m (41ft 7in)**	Bomb load: **907kg (2000lb)**
Height: **4.67m (15ft 4in)**	First flight: **October 1939**
Maximum speed: **663km/h (412mph)**	Initial climb: **914m (3000ft) per min**
Service ceiling: **Not Given**	Weight (empty): **4445kg (9800lb)**
Range: **1577km (980 miles)**	Weight (loaded): **6010kg (13,250lb)**

Although schemed as a high-performance interceptor to replace the Spitfire and Hurricane, the Typhoon proved both inadequate in this role and difficult to develop and was evolved as a ground-attack fighter. In this role the Typhoon excelled. Planned in two forms with the Napier Sabre liquid-cooled H-type engine and the Bristol Centaurus air-cooled radial engine – the latter becoming the Tempest – and first flown in prototype form on 24 February 1940, the Typhoon did not fly in Mk IA production form (105 aircraft) until May 1941 and entered service in June the same year. Initially it appeared a failure due to structural weakness in the tail and wholly indifferent performance at altitude as a result of its thick wing. The Mk IB that followed was the definitive version of the Typhoon. It had fixed forward-firing armament of four 20mm cannon, a clear-view sliding bubble canopy and the unreliable Sabre I engine replaced by the more powerful and reliable Sabre II with four- rather than three-blade propeller and later two underwing hardpoints for bombs or drop tanks and, from 1943, rail units for the carriage of four 76mm (3in) unguided air-to-surface rockets. Although hard to aim, these were used to devastating effect in attacks on trains, armour and light shipping, and in the fighting that followed D-Day the Typhoon was a decisive weapon.

SHORT STIRLING

Although in appearance an extremely impressive aircraft, with vast length, unprecedented height and even two separate tailwheels, the Stirling was unpopular with the men who flew it. The design was completed in 1938 to Specification B.12/36, which called for a seven/eight-man crew heavy bomber. The prototype flew in May 1939, and in August 1940 the first production aircraft began to be delivered, marking the entry into service of the first four-engined heavy bomber for RAF Bomber Command. The Air Ministry's demand for a span of less than 30.48m (100ft) meant that in service the Stirling suffered from poor ceiling and sluggish manoeuvrability. Although it carried a relatively heavy bomb load, it could not carry bombs any bigger than 907kg (2000lb) – the largest size when the design was completed in 1938. Operations began with daylight attacks in February 1941, soon switched to night, and by 1943 the Stirling was used mainly as a glider tug, transport and carrier of ECM jamming and spoofing devices for 100 Group.

The 2374 aircraft produced included 756 Mk I bombers with 1189kW (1595hp) Hercules XI engines, 875 Mk III bombers with a revised dorsal turret, 579 Mk IV paratroop and glider-towing aircraft without nose and dorsal turrets, and 160 Mk V unarmed transports.

SPECIFICATIONS

SHORT STIRLING

Manufacturer: **Short Bros., Ltd.**	Crew: **7/8**
Type: **Heavy Bomber**	Powerplant: **4 x Bristol Hercules XVI**
Length: **26.59m (87ft 3in)**	Armament: **7 x 0.303in MG**
Span: **30.20m (99ft 1in)**	Bomb load: **6350kg (14,000lb)**
Height: **6.93m (22ft 9in)**	First flight: **14 May 1939**
Maximum speed: **434km/h (270mph)**	Initial climb: **244m (800ft) per min**
Service ceiling: **Not Given**	Weight (empty): **21,274kg (46,900lb)**
Range: **3235km (2010 miles)**	Weight (loaded): **31,752kg (70,000lb)**

SHORT SUNDERLAND

SPECIFICATIONS

SHORT SUNDERLAND

Manufacturer: **Short Bros., Ltd.**	Crew: **10**
Type: **Maritime Recon'**	Powerplant: **4 x Bristol Pegasus XXII**
Length: **26.00m (85ft 3.5in)**	Armament: **8 x 0.303in MG**
Span: **34.38m (112ft 9.5in)**	Bomb load: **907kg (2000lb)**
Height: **10.52m (34ft 6in)**	First flight: **16 October 1937**
Maximum speed: **336km/h (209mph)**	Initial climb: **220m (720ft) per min**
Service ceiling: **4570m (15,000ft)**	Weight (empty): **13,875kg (30,589lb)**
Range: **4023km (2500 miles)**	Weight (loaded): **22,226kg (49,000lb)**

Short had over two decades experience in seaplane and flying boat building when it undertook to design and develop a military, general reconnaissance flying boat for the Air Ministry, which the company derived from S.23 "Empire" class boats. An order for 21 production examples of the S.25 was placed in March 1936, some 18 months before the prototype made its maiden flight in October 1937. The initial production model was the Sunderland Mk I that entered service in summer 1938; by the time war had broken out, four British-based squadrons had converted onto the type. Sunderland Mk I production totalled 90, powered by 753kW (1010hp) Bristol Pegasus engines.

The Sunderland Mk II had more powerful (783kW/1050hp) Bristol Pegasus XVIII radial engines and, later in the production run, a twin-gun dorsal turret in place of the single port and starboard waist-mounted weapons, and the addition of air-to-surface search radar. First flown in June 1942, the Sunderland Mk III was the first major production model of the family and was in essence a late-production Sunderland Mk II with a revised planing hull. The last production model was the Sunderland GR.Mk V, of which 143 were completed up to June 1946 with a significantly improved powerplant, better armament and detail modifications.

SUPERMARINE SEAFIRE

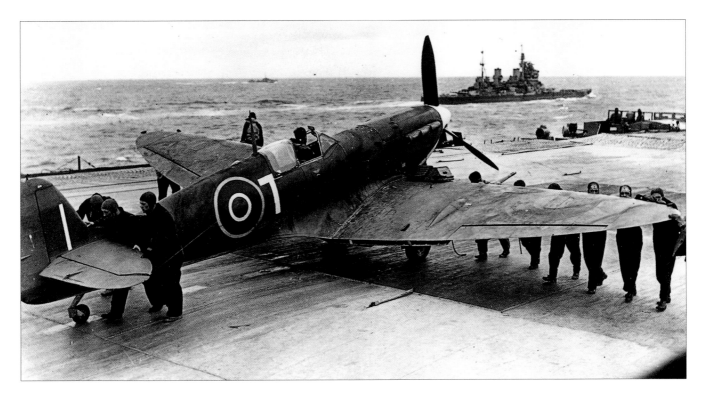

In 1940 the Royal Navy had no better carrier-borne fighter aircraft than the Blackburn Skua, and even with the expected service entry of its Fairey Fulmar replacement the service was faced with the technical and tactical obsolescence of its carrier-borne fighter force. In response, the RN ordered the Seafire, a navalized version of the Spitfire with arrestor gear and catapult spools, for service from June 1942.

The main variants were the Seafire Mk IB (166 conversions from Spitfire Mk VB standard), Seafire Mk IIC (372 aircraft equipped with cannon armament and bombs racks for low- and medium-altitude operations as well as reconnaissance-fighter operations), and the definitive Seafire Mk III (1220 aircraft in the same variants as the Seafire Mk II but with folding wings). There were also 30 Seafire Mk III (Hybrid) aircraft with fixed wings, these later being reclassified as Seafire Mk IIC machines, and the Seafire Mks XV, XVII, 45, 46 and 47 which were post-war developments.

The Seafire offered good performance, but was hampered for carrier-borne operations by its long nose and narrow-track main landing gear units. There were numerous post-war developments of the aircraft, the last of which was finally retired from service with the Royal Navy Volunteer Reserve (RNVR) in 1967.

SPECIFICATIONS

SUPERMARINE SEAFIRE

Manufacturer: **Supermarine Aviation**	Crew: **One**
Type: **Carrier-Borne Fighter**	Powerplant: **1 x RR Merlin 55M**
Length: **9.21m (30ft 2.5in)**	Armament: **2 x cannon, 4 x MG**
Span: **11.23m (36ft 10in)**	Bomb load: **227kg (500lb)**
Height: **3.42m (11ft 2.5in)**	First flight: **Not Given**
Maximum speed: **560km/h (348mph)**	Initial climb: **762m (2501ft) per min**
Service ceiling: **7315m (24,000ft)**	Weight (empty): **2814kg (6204lb)**
Range: **890km (553 miles)**	Weight (loaded): **3465kg (7640lb)**

SUPERMARINE SPITFIRE Mk I

SPECIFICATIONS

SUPERMARINE SPITFIRE Mk I

Manufacturer: **Supermarine Aviation**	Crew: **One**
Type: **Fighter, Fighter-Bomber**	Powerplant: **1 x RR Merlin 45**
Length: **9.12m (29ft 11in)**	Armament: **8 x 0.303in MG**
Span: **11.23m (36ft 10in)**	Bomb load: **227kg (500lb)**
Height: **3.02m (9ft 11in)**	First flight: **5 March 1936**
Maximum speed: **594km/h (394mph)**	Initial climb: **1204m (3950ft) per min**
Service ceiling: **11,125m (36,500ft)**	Weight (empty): **2267kg (4998lb)**
Range: **1827km (1,135 miles)**	Weight (loaded): **2911kg (6417lb)**

When he began designing the Spitfire in the mid-1930s, R.J. Mitchell could hardly have known that he was creating one of the most famous of all aircraft. Mitchell brought to the project valuable experience gained through the Schneider Trophy races, and fortunately had a virtually free rein when creating the Spitfire. The aircraft, known initially as the Type 300, was developed around the Rolls-Royce PV 12 (later Merlin) engine, and the prototype was subsequently ordered into production in June 1936 as the Spitfire Mk I. Service deliveries of 310 Mk I aircraft began in July 1938 and at the outbreak of war the RAF had some 18 squadrons of them.

The Spitfire's reputation was cemented during the Battle of Britain, and although less numerous than the Hurricane it proved a better match for the Bf 109E owing to its exceptional manoeuvrability. The Mk I was followed by 1566 IBs with twin 20mm cannon, the Mk IIA and IIB with Merlin XII, the one-off experimental Mk III with Merlin XX, the Mk IV, 229 photo-reconnaissance versions of the Spitfire Mk V, and then by the Mk V with strengthened fuselage for Merlin 45 or Merlin 50 engines, drop tanks and bomb provision. Suffix LF designated an aircraft with the low-altitude clipped wing and F the standard wing. A, B and C were all different armament fits.

SUPERMARINE SPITFIRE PR Mk XI

When introduced into service in early 1941 the Focke Wulf Fw 190 immediately proved itself superior to any British fighter and Supermarine urgently sought ways of improving the performance of the Spitfire to counter it. In June 1942 the Mk XI entered service, supposedly as an "interim" measure before other more capable versions became available, but in the event it proved one of the most successful of all Spitfire variants. The Mk XI was in effect really just the airframe of the Spitfire Mk VC (Spitfire Mk V with two cannon and two machine-guns and provision for carrying bombs) with the uprated Merlin 60 series of engines. Production totalled 5665 aircraft in low-, medium- and high-altitude sub-variants; the Spitfire LF.Mk XVI (1054 aircraft) was a development with the 1178kW (1580hp) Packard Merlin 266.

There were also photo-reconnaissance versions such as the Spitfire PR.Mks IX, X and XI, succeeding earlier Spitfire photo-reconnaissance adaptations: the PR.Mk IX was converted from the Mk IX fighter, but the 16 and 471 PR.Mks X and XI were new-build aircraft with Merlin 61, 63 or 70 engines. The 16 PR Mk Xs had a pressurized cockpit and increased fuel tankage; the PR XI was essentially the same but was unpressurized and was the mainstay of the RAF PR units from 1943 to 1945.

SPECIFICATIONS

SUPERMARINE SPITFIRE PR Mk XI

Manufacturer: **Supermarine Aviation**	Crew: **One**
Type: **Fighter, Fighter-Bomber**	Powerplant: **1 x RR Merlin 61**
Length: **9.46m (31ft)**	Armament: **2 x cannon, 4 x MG**
Span: **11.23m (36ft 10in)**	Bomb load: **454kg (1000lb)**
Height: **3.85m (12ft 7.75in)**	First flight: **1942**
Maximum speed: **655km/h (408mph)**	Initial climb: **1204m (3950ft) per min**
Service ceiling: **12,105m (43,000ft)**	Weight (empty): **2545kg (5610lb)**
Range: **1576km (980 miles)**	Weight (loaded): **4309kg (9500lb)**

SUPERMARINE WALRUS

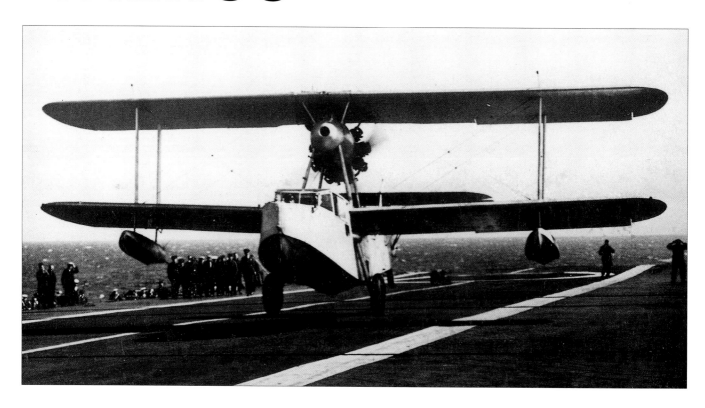

SPECIFICATIONS

SUPERMARINE WALRUS

Manufacturer: **Supermarine Aviation**	Crew: **Four**
Type: **Spotter Amphibian**	Powerplant: **1 x Bristol Pegasus VI**
Length: **11.35m (37ft 3in)**	Armament: **3 x 0.303in MG**
Span: **13.97m (45ft 10in)**	Bomb load: **272kg (600lb)**
Height: **4.65m (15ft 3in)**	First flight: **Not Given**
Maximum speed: **217km/h (135mph)**	Initial climb: **Not Available**
Service ceiling: **5210m (17,100ft)**	Weight (empty): **2223kg (4900lb)**
Range: **966km (600 miles)**	Weight (loaded): **3266kg (7200lb)**

The Walrus was evolved from the Supermarine Seal, a three-man deck-landing amphibian aircraft ordered by the Royal Air Force for use as a fleet spotter to operate from Royal Navy aircraft carriers. A converted Seal II became the prototype Seagull, a folding-wing biplane with retractable landing gear that came into service in the early 1920s.

The prototype Mk V version of the Seagull was fitted with a Bristol Pegasus engine in a pusher configuration and was stressed for catapult-launching. After evaluation by the Fleet Air Arm this version was adopted under the name Walrus Mk I as standard equipment for the Royal Navy's catapult-equipped ships. Production began in 1936 of an eventual 746 "boats", this total including 191 Walrus Mk IIs with a Saro wooden hull and Bristol Pegasus VI engine.

The Walrus saw extensive service in World War II, flying with the Australian, British and New Zealand navies. Known universally as the "Shagbat", the Supermarine Walrus was also used in the air-sea rescue role, ensuring it a place in the hearts of many aircrew. It was superseded in service from 1944 by the Sea Otter, which was essentially a Walrus airframe with a tractor engine, and the last biplane to enter service with the Fleet Air Arm.

VICKERS WELLESLEY

Vickers built a large biplane to meet the RAF's G.4/31 Specification that called for a general-purpose and torpedo bomber, but it was so uninspiring that the company decided to build at its own risk a monoplane using the radical and innovative geodetic structure pioneered by Dr Barnes Wallis on the company's airships. The Wellesley emerged for its first flight in June 1935 as a fabric-covered cantilever monoplane with a wing of high aspect ratio and it proved so dramatically superior that the Air Ministry lost its fear of monoplanes and ordered 96 Wellesley Mk I aircraft, optimized for the medium-bomber role with the bombs carried in two underwing panniers. The Mk I entered service in April 1937, and production up to May 1938 totalled 176 aircraft, most of the later aircraft being completed (unofficially designated Mk II) with a continuous "glasshouse" canopy bridging the front and rear cockpits. The aircraft was distinguished by the very long-span wing, extreme cruise efficiency and a reliable engine, prompting the establishment of the Long Range Development Flight that made a number of record-breaking flights, one of them a 48-hour non-stop trip from Ismalia, Egypt, to Darwin, Australia – a distance of some 11,525km (7162 miles). The Wellesley saw useful service during the first part of the war until late 1942.

SPECIFICATIONS

VICKERS WELLESLEY

Manufacturer: **Vickers-Armstrong Ltd**	Crew: **Two**
Type: **General-Purpose Bomber**	Powerplant: **1 x Bristol Pegasus XX**
Length: **11.96m (39ft 3in)**	Armament: **2 x 0.303in MG**
Span: **22.73m (74ft 7in)**	Bomb load: **907kg (2000lb)**
Height: **3.75m (12ft 4in)**	First flight: **9 June 1935**
Maximum speed: **369km/h (228mph)**	Initial climb: **366m (1200ft) per min**
Service ceiling: **10,060m (33,000ft)**	Weight (empty): **2889kg (6369lb)**
Range: **1786km (1110 miles)**	Weight (loaded): **5035kg (11,100lb)**

VICKERS WELLINGTON

SPECIFICATIONS

VICKERS WELLINGTON

Manufacturer: **Vickers-Armstrong Ltd.**	Crew: **Six**
Type: **Medium Bomber**	Powerplant: **2 x Bristol Hercules**
Length: **19.68m (64ft 7in)**	Armament: **7 x 0.303in MG**
Span: **26.26m (86ft 2in)**	Bomb load: **2041kg (4500lb)**
Height: **5.31m (17ft 5in)**	First flight: **15 June 1936**
Maximum speed: **410km/h (255mph)**	Initial climb: **320m (1050ft) per min**
Service ceiling: **6705m (22,000ft)**	Weight (empty): **10,194kg (22,474lb)**
Range: **3033km (1885 miles)**	Weight (loaded): **16,556kg (36,500lb)**

The geodetic construction successfully employed on the Wellesley was used again on the Wellington, which bore the brunt of the bomber effort in the early stages of the war until large numbers of four-engined heavy bombers became available. There were some difficulties in applying it to wings, cut-out nacelles and fuselages with large bomb doors but the prototype demonstrated good performance and the type was put into service in October 1938. The initial model was the Wellington Mk I with 746kW (1000hp) Pegasus XVIII radial engines. Development as a bomber continued via the Mk III with Rolls-Royce Merlin Vee engines, Mk III with Hercules III or XI radial engines, Mk IV with Pratt & Whitney Twin Wasp radial engines, Mk VI with Merlin engines, and Mk X with Hercules engines.

As the Wellington became obsolescent in the bomber role it found increasing employment as a maritime type for Coastal Command. The specialized variant was the Wellington GR.Mk VIII, a development of the Mk IC bomber with either ASV.Mk II radar or a Leigh Light for anti-ship and anti-submarine operations, and which entered service in spring 1942. The following GR.Mks XI, XII, XIII and XIV had different engine and radar fits for anti-shipping anti-submarine, mine clearance and transport work.

WESTLAND LYSANDER

Resulting from a 1934 requirement for a battlefield reconnaissance and army cooperation aircraft, the distinctive Lysander was designed to provide its two-man crew with the best possible fields of vision to the front and sides, especially towards the ground, and was therefore planned as a high-wing cabin monoplane with a substantial fuselage carrying a large glazed cockpit. The prototype first flew in June 1936, and when it entered service in June 1938 it was used for artillery spotting and message pick-ups. However, in wartime the Lysander blossomed into a remarkable multi-role aircraft. The first He 111 to be shot down in BEF territory fell to the modestly armed Lysander, and during the battle for France it was operated as a night-fighter and ground-attack aircraft, also making precision supply drops over Calais. Production versions were the Lysander Mk I (169), Lysander Mk II (517) with the 675kW (905hp) Bristol Perseus XII engine, Lysander Mk III (517) with the Mercury XX engine, and Mk IIIA (347) – an improved version of the Mk III. From 1941 it was increasingly used as a target-tug (100 new TT.Mk IIIA aircraft with 70 conversions) and to deliver agents into Europe; the best known variant was probably the IIISCW, used for agent-insertion or -recovery, which had a belly tank and ladder to provide access to the lofty cockpit.

SPECIFICATIONS

WESTLAND LYSANDER

Manufacturer: **Westland Aircraft Ltd.**	*Crew:* **1/2**
Type: **Tactical Reconnaissance**	*Powerplant:* **1 x Bristol Mercury XII**
Length: **9.30m (30ft 6in)**	*Armament:* **3 x 0.303in MG**
Span: **15.24m (50ft)**	*Bomb load:* **227kg (500lb)**
Height: **3.35m (11ft)**	*First flight:* **15 June 1936**
Maximum speed: **369km/h (229mph)**	*Initial climb:* **580m (1900ft) per min**
Service ceiling: **7925m (26,000ft)**	*Weight (empty):* **1844kg (4065lb)**
Range: **966km (600 miles)**	*Weight (loaded):* **3402kg (7500lb)**

BREDA Ba 65

SPECIFICATIONS

BREDA Ba 65

Manufacturer:
Societa Ernesto Breda

Type:
Ground-Attack

Length:
9.30m (30ft 6.25in)

Span:
12.10m (39ft 8.5in)

Height:
3.20m (10ft 6in)

Maximum speed:
430km/h (267mph)

Service ceiling:
6300m (20,670ft)

Range:
550km (342 miles)

Crew:
One

Powerplant:
1 x Fiat A.80 RC.41

Armament:
4 x MG

Bomb load:
500kg (1102lb)

First flight:
September 1935

Initial climb:
Not Available

Weight (empty):
2400kg (5291lb)

Weight (loaded):
2950kg (6504lb)

Breda began building aircraft in 1917 and soon grew into one of the largest Italian aeronautical concerns. The Ba 65 was schemed as a multi-role warplane capable of fulfilling the roles of interceptor, light bomber or reconnaissance/attack aircraft. The prototype flew in September 1935 in the form of a low-wing monoplane of all-metal construction (except for the fabric-covered trailing edges). The Regia Aeronautica ordered 81 of the aircraft equipped with the French Gnome-Rhône radial engine that had been fitted to the prototype. An initial batch of 13 single-seat aircraft were sent for evaluation in Spain with the Aviazione Legionare; operational experience there revealed that the Ba 65 was only suitable for the attack role and it was thereafter seconded to the assault wings (stormi).

A second batch of 137 aircraft was delivered between 1938 and July 1939, this total included some that were fitted with an open observer's station above the trailing edge of the rear wing, and a small number fitted with a Breda L turret. Both had a single 7.7mm machine-gun in this position. During the early days of the war over the North African desert, Ba 65s were pitched against the British Royal Air Force, but suffered from appalling reliability problems and by February 1941 no serviceable examples remained.

CAPRONI Ca 133

As Mussolini's Italy began to expand by restoring the "lost colonies" and forcibly building up an overseas empire, a need arose for an aircraft suitable for operations in these new territories; one in the mould of the British Vickers Vincent and Westland Wapiti. The Societa Italiana Caproni produced the Ca 101 to meet this need, with at least 200 being delivered in the early 1930s to serve as bomber, troop-carrier, reconnaissance, ground-attack and supply aircraft. This was followed by the Ca 111, with an uprated powerplant, which served in Ethiopia and Albania – and in 1935 by the Ca 133 which introduced a number of drag-lowering features, namely neat long-chord cowlings (housing three uprated engines), together with faired legs and spatted wheels for the main landing gear units, an improved tail unit and split flaps on the wing trailing edges. The Italian air force soon realized that despite its improvements the type was suitable only for colonial use in North and East Africa. At the outbreak of war it equipped 14 Squadriglie di Bombardimento in these theatres. Ca 133 production totalled 419 aircraft, and conversions included 21 Ca 133S air ambulances and 329 Ca 133T transports with reduced armament. The Ca 133 suffered heavy losses at the hands of British fighters, although some found their way to the Russian Front after Italy's capitulation in 1943.

SPECIFICATIONS

CAPRONI Ca 133

Manufacturer: **Societa Italiana Caproni**	Crew: **Three**
Type: **Bomber and Transport**	Powerplant: **3 x Piaggio Stella PVII**
Length: **15.36m (50ft 4.75in)**	Armament: **4 x 7.7mm MG**
Span: **21.24m (68ft 8in)**	Bomb load: **1200kg (2646lb)**
Height: **4.00m (13ft 1in)**	First flight: **1935**
Maximum speed: **265km/h (165mph)**	Initial climb: **Not Available**
Service ceiling: **5500m (18,045ft)**	Weight (empty): **4190kg (9237lb)**
Range: **1350km (838 miles)**	Weight (loaded): **6700kg (14,771lb)**

MACCHI 202 FOLGORE

SPECIFICATIONS

MACCHI 202 FOLGORE

Manufacturer: **Aeronautica Macchi**	Crew: **One**
Type: **Interceptor Fighter**	Powerplant: **1 x Alfa Romeo RC 41-1**
Length: **8.85m (29ft 0.5in)**	Armament: **2 x 12.7mm MG**
Span: **10.58m (34ft 8.5in)**	Bomb load: **None**
Height: **3.04m (9ft 11.5in)**	First flight: **10 August 1940**
Maximum speed: **595km/h (370mph)**	Initial climb: **Not Available**
Service ceiling: **11,500m (37,730ft)**	Weight (empty): **2350kg (5181lb)**
Range: **765km (475 miles)**	Weight (loaded): **3010kg (6636lb)**

The finest Italian fighters of World War II all came from a team led by Mario Castoldi at Macchi of Varese. The company had gained great experience from their involvement in the Schneider Trophy races, yet their first low-wing fighter, the MC.200, was both underpowered and underarmed. Castoldi remained confident in the basic design, but was convinced that its full potential could only be realized with more engine power. Daimler-Benz DB 601A engines were sourced from Germany and fitted to the aircraft to produce the MC.202 Folgore prototype, which first flew in August 1940. Rushed into production, the MC.202 had a new fuselage for the imported engine and a larger cockpit.

Alfa Romeo subsequently acquired a licence to build the powerplant, but the limited availability of this meant that production was slow and totalled only some 1500 aircraft. A further improved version of the same airframe was the MC.205V Veltro, which first flew in April 1942 with a licence-built version of the DB 605 engine and began operations in July 1943. Later machines had 20mm cannon rather than 7.7mm machine-guns in the wings, and most of the 265-odd aircraft served with Aeronautica Nazionale Republicana after Italy's 1943 armistice with the Allies. A high-altitude version existed only in prototype – the MC.205N Orione.

SAVOIA-MARCHETTI SM 79 SPARVIERO

Often derided by uninformed observers, the SM 79 was a fine and robust bomber that unfailingly operated in difficult conditions and is recognized as one of the finest torpedo bombers of World War II. The *Sparviero* (Sparrowhawk) was first flown in 1934 as the SM.79P civil transport prototype with accommodation for eight-passengers. Painted in both civil and military liveries and fitted with various engines, the prototype set numerous world records in 1935–36. Subsequently it was developed as a medium reconnaissance bomber with an uprated powerplant of three Alfa Romeo 126 radial engines and a large ventral gondola.

Production examples of this SM.79-I entered service in late 1936, and established an excellent reputation with the Aviacon Legionaria in Spain. However, the SM 79 was most successfully employed in the role of torpedo bomber, the first dedicated variant being the SM.79-II (two 450mm torpedoes and a powerplant of three 746kW/1000hp Piaggio P.XI RC.40 or 768kW/1030hp Fiat A.80 RC.41 radial engines). The final Italian model was the SM.79-II, an improved SM.79-II with heavier defensive armament but no ventral gondola. Deliveries to the Regia Aeronautica totalled 1230 aircraft, and about 100 others were exported in a number of twin-engined forms.

SPECIFICATIONS

SAVOIA-MARCHETTI SM 79 SPARVIERO

Manufacturer: **Savoia Marchetti**	Crew: **4/5**
Type: **Medium Recon' Bomber**	Powerplant: **3 x Alfa Romeo RC.34**
Length: **15.62m (51ft 3.1in**	Armament: **4 x MG**
Span: **21.20m (69ft 2.7in)**	Bomb load: **2756lb (1250kg)**
Height: **4.40m (14ft 5.25in)**	First flight: **Late 1934**
Maximum speed: **430km/h (267mph)**	Initial climb: **253m (830ft) per min**
Service ceiling: **6500m (21,325ft)**	Weight (empty): **6800kg (14,991lb)**
Range: **1900km (1181 miles)**	Weight (loaded): **10,480kg (23,104lb)**

KAWANISHI E7K "ALF"

SPECIFICATIONS

KAWANISHI E7K2 "ALF"

Manufacturer: **Kawanishi**	Crew: **Three**
Type: **Recon' Floatplane**	Powerplant: **1 x Mitsubishi Zuisei 11**
Length: **10.50m (34ft 5.5in)**	Armament: **3 x MG**
Span: **14m (45ft 11.25in)**	Bomb load: **120kg (265lb)**
Height: **4.85m (15ft 10.5in)**	First flight: **August 1938**
Maximum speed: **275km/h (171mph)**	Initial climb: **Not Available**
Service ceiling: **7060m (23,165ft)**	Weight (empty): **2100kg (4630lb)**
Range: **not available**	Weight (loaded): **3300kg (7275lb)**

In 1932 the Imperial Japanese Navy contracted Kawanishi Kokuki Kabushiki Kaisha for a prototype of its E7K1, the proposed replacement for the E5K then in service. The newer aircraft was a three-seat biplane of unequal span powered by a 462kW (620hp) engine and which was first flown in February 1933. The prototype was handed over to the navy's aircraft evaluation unit in May and flown in a series of competitive service trials against the Aichi B-6.

The Kawanishi type was subsequently ordered into production in May 1934 and the first examples rolled out of the factory early the next year. In service it proved popular on account of its stable and predictable handling characteristics, although the aircraft was somewhat let down by the unreliability of the Hiro engine. Substituting the -91 version of the engine in later aircraft did not cure the problem and for the following E7K2 the manufacturer adopted a Mitsubishi Zuisei 11 radial piston engine (649kW/870hp).

First flown in this form in August 1938, the E7K2 was adopted and entered service in early 1939. By the time that war had broken out in the Pacific in December 1941, most of the 183 E7K1 produced had been relegated to training duties, although the 350 E7K2 aircraft were active until 1943.

KAWASAKI Ki 61 "TONY"

Kawasaki Kokuyu Kogyo Kabushiki Kaisha purchased a licence to produce the German DB 601 in 1937 and revised and lightened it to produce the Ha-40. The Ki-60 low-wing monoplane fighter was planned around this, but proved disappointing and work focused on a lighter fighter identified as the Ki-61 *Hien* (Swallow), unique among Japan's first-line warplanes in being powered by an inverted-Vee piston engine. The first of 12 prototype and pre-production aircraft flew in December 1941, and revealed good performance and handling, reaching a top speed of some 592km/h (368mph). The prototype was tested extensively during the following spring against captured examples of the P-40E and a Bf 109 sent from Germany, along with 800 Mauser MG 151 cannon that were fitted to early production aircraft despite the unreliability of the supply of the electrically fused ammunition. The Ki-61-I entered service in February 1943 and first saw combat in New Guinea in April 1943. Some 1380 aircraft were delivered in two sub-variants differentiated by their armament, followed by 1274 Ki-61 Kai fighters with a lengthened fuselage and different armament. Further development resulted in the Ki-61-II Kai, optimized for high-altitude operations with the unreliable Kawasaki Ha-140 engine, in two sub-variants again distinguishable by armament fit.

SPECIFICATIONS

KAWASAKI Ki 61 "TONY"

Manufacturer:
Kawasaki

Type:
(Ki-61-Ib) Fighter

Length:
8.75m (28ft 8.5in)

Span:
12.10m (39ft 4.25in)

Height:
3.70m (12ft 1.75in)

Maximum speed:
592km/h (368mph)

Service ceiling:
11,600m (37,730ft)

Range:
1100km (684 miles)

Crew:
One

Powerplant:
1 x Kawasaki Ha-40

Armament:
4 x 12.7mm MG

Bomb load:
None

First flight:
December 1941

Initial climb:
675m (2200ft) per min

Weight (empty):
2210kg (4872lb)

Weight (loaded):
3250kg (7165lb)

MITSUBISHI A6M ZERO-SEN

SPECIFICATIONS

MITSUBISHI A6M ZERO-SEN

Manufacturer:
Mitsubishi

Crew:
One

Type:
Fighter, Fighter-Bomber

Powerplant:
1 x Nakajima NK1C

Length:
9.06m (29ft 8.75in)

Armament:
2 x cannon, 2 x MG

Span:
12.00m (39ft 4.5in)

Bomb load:
120kg (265lb)

Height:
3.05m (10ft)

First flight:
1 April 1939

Maximum speed:
534km/h (332mph)

Initial climb:
1370m (4500ft) per min

Service ceiling:
10,000m (32,810ft)

Weight (empty):
1680kg (3704lb)

Range:
3104km (1929 miles)

Weight (loaded):
2796kg (6164lb)

This most famous of all Japanese combat aircraft was developed to a tough 1937 Imperial Japanese Navy requirement, and although it entered service in summer 1940 and was used in the Manchurian campaign neither British nor American staff appear to have been aware of it (this despite the reports of the Flying Tigers volunteer force). The aircraft provided a rude shock at Pearl Harbor and Singapore, for it possessed performance equal and greater to any land-based fighter in the Pacific theatre – at that time a remarkable achievement for a carrier-based fighter. When fitted with a centreline drop tank the Zero had phenomenal range, afforded by sophisticated engine/propeller management techniques.

The A6M was generally known in the West as the Zero, a name derived from its Japanese name *Reisen* (meaning "zero fighter") that resulted from its adoption in the Japanese year 2600 (1940). Lack of a successor meant that the Zero was maintained in development and production (11,280 aircraft) past its effective limits. The type reached its apogee as a dogfighter in the A6M2, while the A6M3 had greater power but shorter range, the A6M5 heavier firepower and the A6M6 better protection and greater fighter-bomber capability. After the Battle of Midway the A6M found itself increasingly outclassed and most ended up as kamikaze aircraft.

MITSUBISHI G4M "BETTY"

The G4M was the Imperial Japanese Navy air force's premier heavy bomber in World War II, yet the insistence in the 1938 specification to which it was built that the aircraft should have a range of 3700km (2000 miles) with a full bomb load meant that reducing its weight took priority over defence and the aircraft was subsequently highly vulnerable (and thus unpopular). Armour plating, self-sealing fuel tanks and a sturdy structure able to absorb battle damage were all sacrificed in the drive to attain acceptable range. The first of two G4M1 prototypes flew in October 1939, and the type entered service early in 1941. Production totalled 1200 G4M1 aircraft in variants such as the Convoy Fighter Escort (five 20mm trainable cannon), Model 11 Attack Bomber and Model 12 Attack Bomber, the last with MK4E engines. Trainer and transport variants were then created as conversions. The G4M2 entered service from mid-1943 with an uprated powerplant, a laminar-flow wing, a larger tailplane, additional fuel capacity and heavier defensive armament for better overall capability, but only at the cost of reduced agility. Recognition of the vulnerability of the aircraft brought the G4M3 with armoured crew areas and a wing revised with self-sealing tanks, but too late to be of any real use. Only 60 had been completed before Japan's surrender in 1945.

SPECIFICATIONS

MITSUBISHI G4M

Manufacturer: **Mitsubishi**	Crew: **Seven**
Type: **Medium Bomber**	Powerplant: **2 x Mitsubishi MK4A**
Length: **20.00m (65ft 7.25in)**	Armament: **1 x cannon, 2 x MG**
Span: **25.00m (82ft 0.25in)**	Bomb load: **800kg (1764lb)**
Height: **6.00m (19ft 8.25in)**	First flight: **October 1939**
Maximum speed: **428km/h (266mph)**	Initial climb: **550m (1800ft) per min**
Service ceiling: **Not Available**	Weight (empty): **6800kg (14,991lb)**
Range: **6033km (3749 miles)**	Weight (loaded): **9500kg (20,944lb)**

BOEING B-17 FLYING FORTRESS

SPECIFICATIONS

BOEING B-17 FLYING FORTRESS

Manufacturer: **Boeing Aircraft Company**	Crew: **10**
Type: **(B-17G) Heavy Bomber**	Powerplant: **4 x Wright R-1820-97**
Length: **22.78m (74ft 9 in)**	Armament: **12 x 0.50in MG**
Span: **31.63m (103ft 9.4in)**	Bomb load: **7983kg (17,600lb)**
Height: **5.82m (19ft 1in)**	First flight: **28 July 1935**
Maximum speed: **486km/h (302mph)**	Initial climb: **164m (540ft) per min**
Service ceiling: **10,850m (35,600ft)**	Weight (empty): **44,560lb (20,212kg)**
Range: **2897km (1800 miles)**	Weight (loaded): **72,000lb (32,659kg)**

In May 1934 the US Army Air Corps (USAAC) issued a specification for a multi-engined anti-shipping bomber. In response, Boeing built the Model 299 as a private-venture prototype with provision for a 2177kg (4800lb) bomb load, which was later evaluated as the XB-17. The USAAC was expected to select the twin-engined Martin B-10, but in the event orders were placed for 14 YB-17 and YB-17A service test aircraft later accepted into service as the B-17 and B-17A aircraft. These models were followed by the slightly modified B-17B (nose), B-17C (defensive armament) and B-17D (extra crew member). Some 20 B-17Cs were transferred to the UK as Fortress Mk I machines; most of the B-17D bombers were stationed in the Far East, where about half were destroyed by Japan on 7 December 1941. The first large-scale production model was the B-17E, with a new tail unit for improved, high-altitude stability, and revised defensive armament including a twin-gun tail position and power-operated twin-gun dorsal and ventral turrets. Most widely produced was the B-17F, which introduced a frameless Plexiglas nose and structural strengthening. The final bomber model was the B-17G Flying Fortress, with a power-operated chin turret. Deliveries of 8680 aircraft began in September 1943, these undertaking the weight of the US bomber effort in Europe from 1944.

BOEING B-29 SUPERFORTRESS

The design and development of the Model 345, the B-29, was a huge undertaking. The process began in March 1938 when Boeing submitted a study for a new bomber with pressurized cabin and tricycle landing gear. This evolved into the Model 345 and after 14 months of intensive development and testing of two prototypes an order was placed for 14 YB-29s and 500 production aircraft. The production effort for these aircraft involved Boeing, Bell, North American and General Motors and later Martin. The B-29 was hugely complex and represented a leap forward in terms of engine power, gross weight, wing loading, pressurization, armament, airborne systems and basic structure. Entering service in June 1944, by VJ Day some 3000 aircraft had been built. These were predominantly stationed in the Marianas Islands and used in a campaign of massed high level bombing to neutralize the war-making potential of Japan by burning her cities and crippling her industries. When this failed to force the Japanese to surrender, a B-29 was equipped to drop the atomic weapons that destroyed Hiroshima and Nagasaki on 6 and 9 August 1945. The baseline B-29 (2458 built) was complemented by the B-29A (1119) with a greater span and improved forward dorsal barbette, and the B-29B (310) with reduced defensive armament but a greater bomb load and speed.

SPECIFICATIONS

BOEING B-29 SUPERFORTRESS

Manufacturer: **Boeing Aircraft Company**	Crew: **Nine**
Type: **Long-Range H'vy Bomber**	Powerplant: **4 x Wright R-3350-23**
Length: **30.18m (99ft)**	Armament: **1 x cannon, 8 x MG**
Span: **43.05m (141ft 2.75in)**	Bomb load: **9072kg (20,000lb)**
Height: **9.02m (29ft 7in)**	First flight: **21 September 1942**
Maximum speed: **576km/h (358mph)**	Initial climb: **160m (526ft) per min**
Service ceiling: **9710m (31,850ft)**	Weight (empty): **31,816kg (70,140lb)**
Range: **5830 miles (9382km)**	Weight (loaded): **56,246kg (124,000lb)**

BREWSTER F2S BUFFALO

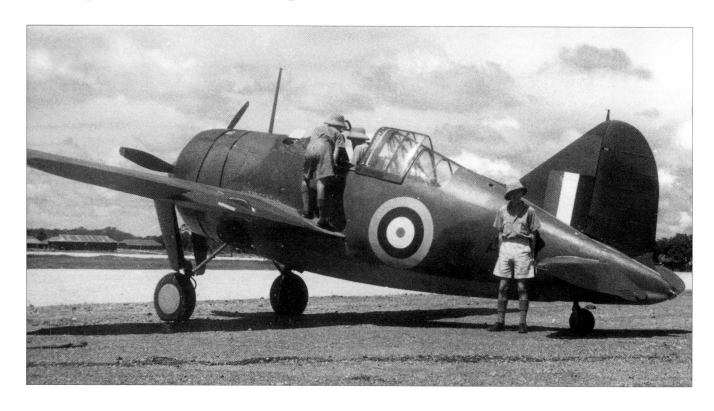

SPECIFICATIONS

BREWSTER F2S BUFFALO

Manufacturer: **Brewster Aeronautical**	Crew: **One**
Type: **Fighter, Fighter-Bomber**	Powerplant: **1 x Wright R-1820-40**
Length: **8.03m (26ft 4in)**	Armament: **4 x 0.50in MG**
Span: **10.67m (35ft)**	Bomb load: **105kg (232lb)**
Height: **3.68m (12ft 1in)**	First flight: **January 1938**
Maximum speed: **517km/h (321mph)**	Initial climb: **698m (2290ft) per min**
Service ceiling: **10,120m (33,200ft)**	Weight (empty): **2146kg (4732lb)**
Range: **2704km (1680 miles)**	Weight (loaded): **3247kg (7159lb)**

The dumpy little Buffalo was one of the first aircraft built by the Brewster Company, which in 1935 secured an order for a US Navy scout-bomber. It also entered a competition for a carrier-based monoplane fighter and won. With such a lack of experience in aircraft design and production, it is not surprising that the first XF2A-1 prototype took almost two years to build. This first flew in January 1938 and in June of that year the Brewster machine was, perhaps surprisingly, selected in preference to the Grumman G.36 Wildcat. Of the 54 F2A-1 production aircraft ordered only 11 entered service on USS *Saratoga* in July 1939 with the 701kW (940hp) R-1820-34 engine (the balance were supplied to Finland).

The US Navy took 43 and 108 examples of the F2A-2 and F2A-3, the former with an uprated engine and armament and the latter with self-sealing tanks and a longer nose. The F2A was generally unsuccessful in American service, but it was also operated by Finland, which was the only country to use the type with major success, Belgium, of which 38 were delivered to the UK as Buffalo Mk Is, the Dutch East Indies, the UK as Buffalo Mk Is, and Australia. In the Pacific the Buffalo fought valiantly against the Japanese, but was outclassed as well as outnumbered and suffered accordingly.

CONSOLIDATED B-24 LIBERATOR

Although conceived some five years after the B-17, the B-24 represented no great improvement over the older aircraft. In fact it was something of a handful for inexperienced pilots, and was also the most complex and expensive combat aircraft built thus far. Yet it was produced in larger numbers (18,431 machines) than any other US warplane of World War II and served on every wartime front and with every Allied nation.

The slightly curious layout was dictated by the need to place the slender wing above the tall fuselage bomb bay. This wing was efficient in cruising flight, which, combined with great fuel capacity, gave the Liberator a longer range than any contemporary landplane. First flown in XB-24 prototype form in December 1939, the first major production models were the B-24D (2738 aircraft), the generally similar B-24E (791 aircraft) and the B-24G (430 aircraft with a power-operated nose turret).

The B-24 made its operational debut in June 1942 with the long-range raids mounted from Egypt against the Ploesti oilfields in Romania. There were other developments, too numerous to list here, which allowed the aircraft to operate on long-range maritime reconnaissance and transport duties, a photo-reconnaissance platform and as a fuel tanker.

SPECIFICATIONS

CONSOLIDATED B-24 LIBERATOR

Manufacturer: **Consolidated Vultee**	Crew: **10**
Type: **Long-Range H'vy Bomber**	Powerplant: **4 x P & W R-1830-43**
Length: **20.22m (66ft 4in)**	Armament: **9 x 0.50in MG**
Span: **33.53m (110ft)**	Bomb load: **3992kg (8800lb)**
Height: **4.46m (17ft 11in)**	First flight: **29 December 1939**
Maximum speed: **488km/h (303mph)**	Initial climb: **274m (900ft) per min**
Service ceiling: **9755m (32,000ft)**	Weight (empty): **14,490kg (32,605lb)**
Range: **4586km (2850 miles)**	Weight (loaded): **27,216kg (60,000lb)**

CONSOLIDATED CATALINA

SPECIFICATIONS

CONSOLIDATED CATALINA

Manufacturer: **Consolidated Vultee**	Crew: **Nine**
Type: **Maritime Recon'**	Powerplant: **2 x P & W R-1830-92**
Length: **19.45m (63ft 10in)**	Armament: **5 x MG**
Span: **31.70m (104ft)**	Bomb load: **2041kg (4500lb)**
Height: **5.76m (18ft 11in)**	First flight: **21 March 1935**
Maximum speed: **288km/h (179mph)**	Initial climb: **158m (518ft) per min**
Service ceiling: **4480m (14,700ft)**	Weight (empty): **9485kg (20,910lb)**
Range: **5713 km (3550 miles)**	Weight (loaded): **16,067kg (35,420lb)**

Against strong competition from Douglas, Consolidated won a 1933 competition to supply the US Navy with its first cantilever monoplane flying boat. The resulting Consolidated PBY series, now universally known as the Catalina after its British designation, has become a classic, built in larger numbers than all other flying boats combined. The XP3Y-1 prototype made its impressive maiden flight in March 1934 and the US Navy subsequently placed a huge order for 60 PBY-1 aircraft. These were followed by 50 PBY-2s, 66 PBY-3s with uprated engines, 33 PBY-4 with further uprated engines and 1024 PBY-5 with still more power and with waist blisters rather than hatches. In 1938 the USSR bought three and urgently tooled up to build an eventual total of more than 400 of its own version.

Retractable tricycle landing gear was introduced in November 1939 with the production designation PBY-5A, of which 794 were delivered to the US Navy. The Royal Air Force received 225 similar PBY-5Bs. Further variants were the PBY-6A (235 machines) with revised armament and a larger tail, and the Naval Aircraft Factory PBN-1 Nomad (156 machines), to a PBY-5A standard but with a larger tail and increased fuel capacity and armament. The PBY's endurance and stability made it ideal for long-range maritime patrol and anti-submarine work.

CURTISS P-40D (KITTYHAWK MK I)

During 1940 Curtiss redesigned the Model 81 in an attempt to improve its performance. The changes included installation of the Allison V-1710-39 engine, allowing the nose to be shortened and the radiator deepened, thus changing the appearance of the aircraft. Additional armour was added, along with an underfuselage hardpoint, and the fuselage guns were deleted; standard armament thereafter was four 0.50in guns in the wings.

The RAF ordered 560 of the improved version in 1940, and it first flew in May 1941 as the Kittyhawk Mk I. Curtiss identified the aircraft as the Hawk 87-A2 and the USAAC, which had ordered the aircraft in September 1940, called it the P-40D. Only 22 of this version were delivered before production for the USAAF switched to the P-40E (Kittyhawk Mk IA), which had two additional wing guns. The next development, the P-40F (Kittyhawk II), involved installing the Packard V-1650 (Rolls-Royce Merlin) engine into a lengthened P-40D fuselage.

Great Britain also purchased, or received under the Lend-Lease scheme, Kittyhawk Mk II to IV variants of the P-40F, K/M and N, each version heavier and thus less manoeuvrable than its predecessor. Some 2097 of the American aircraft were also shipped to the Soviet Union for service on the Eastern Front.

SPECIFICATIONS

CURTISS P-40D (KITTYHAWK MK I)

Manufacturer: **Curtiss-Wright Corp.**	Crew: **One**
Type: **Fighter, Fighter-Bomber**	Powerplant: **1 x Allison V-1710-81**
Length: **10.16m (33ft 4in)**	Armament: **6 x 0.50in MG**
Span: **11.37m (37ft 3.5in)**	Bomb load: **680kg (1500lb)**
Height: **3.23m (10ft 7in)**	First flight: **Not Given**
Maximum speed: **552km/h (343mph)**	Initial climb: **646m (2120ft) per min**
Service ceiling: **9450m (31,000ft)**	Weight (empty): **2812kg (6200lb)**
Range: **1207km (750 miles)**	Weight (loaded): **5171kg (11,400lb)**

CURTISS P-40 (TOMAHAWK MK I)

SPECIFICATIONS

CURTISS P-40B (TOMAHAWK MK I)

Manufacturer: **Curtiss-Wright Corp.**	Crew: **One**
Type: **(P-40B) Fighter**	Powerplant: **1 x Allison V-1710-33**
Length: **9.66 m (31ft 8.5in)**	Armament: **4 x MG**
Span: **11.37m (37ft 3.5in)**	Bomb load: **None**
Height: **3.22m (10ft 7in)**	First flight: **January 1940**
Maximum speed: **567km/h (352mph)**	Initial climb: **807m (2650ft) per min**
Service ceiling: **9875m (32,400ft)**	Weight (empty): **2536kg (5590lb)**
Range: **1513km (940 miles)**	Weight (loaded): **3447kg (7600lb)**

In November 1934 Curtiss began the development of a new "Hawk" fighter with cantilever monoplane wing, retracting landing gear, R-1830 radial engine and all-metal construction. This was put into production as the P-36, which spawned numerous variants including the Hawk 75A export model.

More than 1300 radial-engined models were built before the decision was made to build the P-40 with a liquid-cooled Allison engine. The R-1830 engine was reliable and powerful by the standards of the 1930s, but when it became clear that it lacked the potential for development into more powerful forms Curtiss sought new means of exploiting the Model 75 airframe by installing the 775kW (1040hp) liquid-cooled Allison V-1710 Vee engine. This was particularly significant in a country where aircraft engines had become almost universally air-cooled, and predictably there were many teething troubles.

The first production model was the P-40, which entered service from May 1940. This was followed by the P-40B, P-40C, P-40D and P-40E, as well as Tomahawk Mks I, II and III for the British RAF, Australian RAAF and South African SAAF which were used as low-level army cooperation machines in Britain and as ground-attack fighters in North Africa.

CURTISS SB2C HELLDIVER

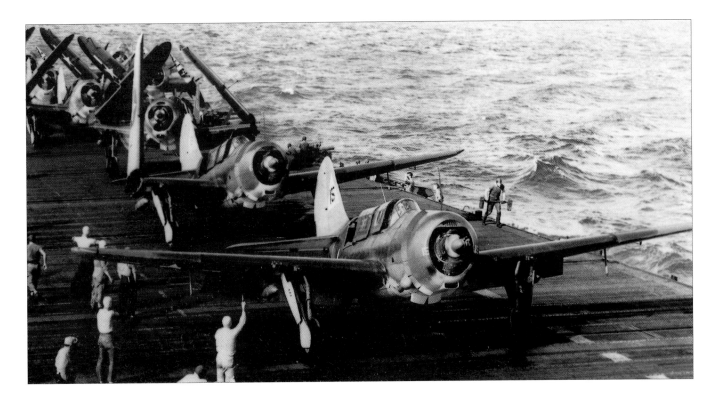

During World War II, by far the most successful Allied dive-bomber was the Douglas SBD Dauntless, which sank more Japanese shipping than any other Allied weapon. The aircraft built to succeed the Dauntless was the SB2C Helldiver, which perpetuated a name established by Curtiss with an earlier series of dive-bombers. This new monoplane had a powerful engine, large folding wing and internal bomb bay, and first flew in XSB2C-1 prototype form in December 1940. Development took a long time, partly because the prototype crashed, but mainly because the US services asked for 880 further major design changes after the SB2C-1 had been frozen for production in November 1941. Built to the extent of 7200 aircraft, including the A-25 land-based version for the US Army as well as the Canadian-built SBF and SBW, the type made its operational debut in November 1943.

In service it was never as effective as its predecessor, but fought in every major conflict of the war in the Pacific. The main models were the SB2C-1 baseline variant (978 aircraft in two sub-variants), SB2C-3 (1112 aircraft) with the 1417kW (1900hp) R-2600-20 engine, SB4C-4 (2045 aircraft in two sub-variants) with provision for additional underwing stores, and the SB2C-5 (970 aircraft) with increased fuel tankage.

SPECIFICATIONS

CURTISS SB2C HELLDIVER

Manufacturer: **Curtiss-Wright Corp.**	*Crew:* **Two**
Type: **Scout and Dive-Bomber**	*Powerplant:* **1 x Wright R-2600-8**
Length: **11.18m (36ft 8in)**	*Armament:* **2 x cannon, 2 x MG**
Span: **15.15m (49ft 8.26in)**	*Bomb load:* **1361kg (3000lb)**
Height: **4.00m (13ft 1.5in)**	*First flight:* **18 December 1940**
Maximum speed: **452km/h (281mph)**	*Initial climb:* **Not Available**
Service ceiling: **7375m (24,200ft)**	*Weight (empty):* **4588kg (10,114lb)**
Range: **2213 km (1375 miles)**	*Weight (loaded):* **7626kg (16,812lb)**

DOUGLAS A-20

SPECIFICATIONS

DOUGLAS A-20

Manufacturer: **Douglas Aircraft Co.**	Crew: **Three**
Type: **Light Attack Bomber**	Powerplant: **2 x Wright R-2600-23**
Length: **14.63m (47ft 11.88in)**	Armament: **9 x 0.50in MG**
Span: **18.69m (61ft 4in)**	Bomb load: **1814kg (4000lb)**
Height: **5.36m (17ft 7in)**	First flight: **26 October 1938**
Maximum speed: **546km/h (339mph)**	Initial climb: **355m (1164ft) per min**
Service ceiling: **7225m (23,700ft)**	Weight (empty): **7708kg (16,993lb)**
Range: **3380km (2100 miles)**	Weight (loaded): **12,338kg (27,200lb)**

As the RAF began daring low-level operations over occupied France with its Boston Mk III aircraft production of the A-20 version of the DB-7 for the USAAC was getting underway. An initial USAAC contract for the DB-7 was placed in May 1939 for 63 A-20 aircraft, which were delivered in the form of 59 P-70 night-fighters, equipped with British radar and four 20mm cannon, and three photo-reconnaissance machines. The A-20A (143 aircraft) that followed was generally similar but had unsupercharged engines and armament revised to six 3in machine-guns. The A-20B had two nose-mounted 0.50in guns and was roughly equivalent to the DB-7A; the A-20C was built to the same standard as the Boston Mk III to help standardization (this version was also supplied to the USSR under Lend-Lease).

A-20Cs undertook the first combat mission by the Eighth Air Force on 4 July 1942. A small number of A-20E conversions were completed, re-equipping A-20As with the A-20B powerplant. The most important model was the A-20G attack bomber, 2850 of which were supplied with a "solid" nose and heavier forward-firing armament, and later a dorsal turret with twin 0.50in machine-guns. There were progressive improvements to all areas and there were A-20H, A-20J and A-20K versions. Total production overall was 7385.

DOUGLAS DC-3

In 1935 Douglas designer Arthur E. Raymond planned the Douglas Sleeper Transport as an enlarged and improved version of the DC-2, with greater power and accommodation increased to 21, but he cannot have realized that as well as becoming the standard airliner of its day, it would also become the most widely used military transport ever. The prototype flew in December 1935, and the first deliveries were to civilian carriers. However, the DC-3 remains better known in its military forms as the USAAC's C-47 Skytrain, US Navy's R4D and the Royal Air Force's Dakota.

Production of these and other military variants in the USA totalled some 10,050 aircraft. The vast majority were the utility C-47 version with a strengthened cargo floor and large double doors, although there were some oddities, such as a glider version and a float-equipped version. The Soviet Union built the aircraft as the Li-2 in numbers totalling more than 2700 aircraft. These aircraft were truly war-winning weapons; Eisenhower said that along with the Jeep, the Bazooka and the Sherman tank, the C-47 had been one of the four decisive weapons of World War II, for it provided the Allies with an unparalleled transport capability that expanded into paratroop and glider-towing capabilities as World War II progressed.

SPECIFICATIONS

DOUGLAS DC-3

Manufacturer: **Douglas Aircraft Co.**	Crew: **2/3**
Type: **Transport**	Powerplant: **2 x P & W R-1830-92**
Length: **19.63m (64ft 5.5in)**	Armament: **None**
Span: **28.90m (95ft 0in)**	Bomb load: **None**
Height: **5.20m (16ft 11in)**	First flight: **17 December 1935**
Maximum speed: **370km/h (230mph)**	Initial climb: **366m (1200ft) per min**
Service ceiling: **7315m (24,000ft)**	Weight (empty): **8103kg (17,865lb)**
Range: **2575km (1600 miles)**	Weight (loaded): **14,061kg (31,000lb)**

DOUGLAS SBD DAUNTLESS

SPECIFICATIONS

DOUGLAS SBD DAUNTLESS

Manufacturer: **Douglas Aircraft Co.**	Crew: **Two**
Type: **Scout and Dive-Bomber**	Powerplant: **1 x Wright R-1820-60**
Length: **10.09m (33ft 1.25in)**	Armament: **4 x MG**
Span: **12.66m (41ft 6.38in)**	Bomb load: **1021kg (2250lb)**
Height: **4.14m (13ft 7in)**	First flight: **23 July 1938**
Maximum speed: **410km/h (255mph)**	Initial climb: **457m (1500ft) per min**
Service ceiling: **7780m (25,530ft)**	Weight (empty): **2905kg (6404lb)**
Range: **2519km (1565 miles)**	Weight (loaded): **4853kg (10,700lb)**

Undeniably the best American dive-bomber of the war, the SBD Dauntless was developed by Northrop and its chief designer Ed Heinemann in 1934 for the American carrier fleet then under construction. The resulting BT-1 design was based on the established Northrop A-17A, and 54 were delivered to the US Navy from November 1937. Features of the aircraft were large perforated split flaps and main gears that retracted back into large fairings. The last aircraft was delivered in October 1938, in much modified form, as the BT-2, with inward-retracting main wheels, a 746kW (1000hp) Cyclone engine and many refinements. Northrop had by this time become part of Douglas Aircraft and production aircraft were designated SBD-1. From June 1940 until it was retired four years later this was one of the most important US types, playing a decisive role at Coral Sea, Midway and the Solomons – despite the fact that it possessed indifferent performance and poor manoeuvrability. The main production models were the SBD-1 (57) with the 746kW (1000hp) R-1820-32 engine, SBD-2 (87) with more armament and fuel, SBD-3 (584) with better machine-guns, self-sealing fuel tankage and 24- rather than 12-volt electrics, SBD-4 (780) with detail improvements, SBD-5 (3025) with greater power, and SBD-6 (451) with a 1007kW (1350hp) R-1820-66 engine.

GRUMMAN TBF AVENGER

As the US Navy's Pacific campaign progressed a very real need for effective torpedo bombers was exposed and in response Grumman design staff under Bill Schwendler quickly developed the TBF Avenger. Two were ordered in April 1940 and the first of two XTBF-1 prototypes made the type's maiden flight in August 1941. Service deliveries began in January 1942, and large numbers were in service in time for the type to make a disastrous combat debut at the Battle of Midway in June 1942. Nevertheless, the TBF rapidly matured as the classic torpedo-bomber of World War II and proved to be a robust and well-equipped aircraft.

Production of the TBF-1 model (the only model that was built) included sub-variants such as the winterized TBF-1J Avenger, TBF-1P photo-reconnaissance type, TBF-1B for the Fleet Air Arm in the UK, TBF-1C with two 0.50in machine-guns in the leading edges of the wing, TBF-1CP photo-reconnaissance type, TBF-1D for the anti-submarine role with radar and underwing rockets, TBF-1E with podded air-to-surface radar, and TBF-1L with a powerful retractable searchlight for night illumination of surface vessels. Production was also undertaken by General Motors Corporation, which produced 7546 of the TBM model in a number of sub-variants, including the TBM-3D with anti-submarine radar.

SPECIFICATIONS

GRUMMAN TBF AVENGER

Manufacturer: **Grumman Aircraft**	Crew: **Three**
Type: **Torpedo-Bomber**	Powerplant: **1 x Wright R-2600-8**
Length: **12.42m (40ft 9in)**	Armament: **4 x MG**
Span: **16.51m (54ft 2in)**	Bomb load: **1134kg (2500lb)**
Height: **4.19m (13ft 9in)**	First flight: **1 August 1941**
Maximum speed: **414km/h (257mph)**	Initial climb: **235m (770ft) per min**
Service ceiling: **6525m (21,400ft)**	Weight (empty): **4788kg (10,555lb)**
Range: **4321km (2685 miles)**	Weight (loaded): **7876kg (17,364lb)**

GRUMMAN F4F WILDCAT

SPECIFICATIONS

GRUMMAN F4F WILDCAT

Manufacturer: **Grumman Aircraft**	Crew: **One**
Type: **Fighter, Fighter-Bomber**	Powerplant: **1 x P & W R-1830-86**
Length: **8.76m (28ft 9in)**	Armament: **6 x 0.50in**
Span: **11.58m (38ft 0in)**	Bomb load: **91kg (200lb)**
Height: **2.81m (9ft 2.5in)**	First flight: **2 September 1937**
Maximum speed: **512km/h (318mph)**	Initial climb: **594m (1950ft) per min**
Service ceiling: **10,365m (34,000ft)**	Weight (empty): **2612kg (5758lb)**
Range: **2012km (1250 miles)**	Weight (loaded): **3607kg (7952lb)**

Designed as a biplane to continue Grumman's very successful F3F series of single-seat carrier fighters, the XF4F-1 biplane was replanned on the drawing board in summer 1936 as a mid-wing monoplane (XF4F-2), first flying in September 1937. It lost out to the Brewster Buffalo in the US Navy fighter competition, but Grumman continued to develop it as the XF4-3 with a more powerful engine, and in early 1939 received an order from the French Aeronavale for 100, the US Navy following with 54 in August. The French aircraft were subsequently diverted to Britain, where they became Martlet Is.

Eventually 284 F4F-3 production aircraft were built, with the R-1830-76 engine. Production built up with both Twin Wasp and Cyclone engines, and included the F4F-3A (95 aircraft), F4F-4 with manually folding wing tips (1144 aircraft) and unarmed photo-reconnaissance F4F-7 (21 aircraft). General Motors built 1140 FM-1 (F4F-4) aircraft and the powerful 4467 FM-2 aircraft with the R-1830-56 engine and a taller fin. Some 1082 F4Fs were delivered to the UK, where the type initially known as the Martlet became the Wildcat. The F4F was the US Navy's most important fighter at the time of the US entry into the war, and was involved in early actions in the Pacific. Production continued right through the war.

LOCKHEED HUDSON

To meet a British and Commonwealth coastal reconnaissance bomber requirement outlined by the British Purchasing Commission in 1938, Lockheed produced a militarized version of its Model 14 Super Electra transport, which the British called the Hudson. The first of 351 Hudson Mk I aircraft reached the UK by sea in February 1939, and entered service in February 1939. On 8 October 1939 a Hudson over Jutland shot down the first German aircraft claimed by the RAF in the war. In February 1940 another Hudson discovered the German prison ship *Altmark* in a Norwegian fjord and directed naval forces to the rescue and over the Dunkirk beaches they were flown as dogfighters. From 1942 Hudsons made numerous clandestine landings in France to deliver or collect agents or supplies.

There were numerous models from the Mk II to Mk VI, distinguished primarily by their engines. Large numbers of Hudsons were also delivered under the Lend-Lease scheme, and variously configured for anti-shipping and submarine work with radar, rocket launchers and depth charges, and for the air-sea rescue mission with an underslung air-dropped lifeboat. Total deliveries were 2584 including about 490 armed versions for the US Army, 20 PBO (Hudson Mk IIIA) for the US Navy and 300 AT-18/-18A gunnery and navigational trainers.

SPECIFICATIONS

LOCKHEED HUDSON

Manufacturer: **Lockheed**	Crew: **Six**
Type: **Coastal Recon' Bomber**	Powerplant: **2 x GR-1820-G102A**
Length: **13.50m (44ft 3.75in)**	Armament: **7 x 0.303in MG**
Span: **19.96m (65ft 6in)**	Bomb load: **612kg (1350lb)**
Height: **3.32m (10ft 10.5in)**	First flight: **10 December 1938**
Maximum speed: **357km/h (222mph)**	Initial climb: **305m (1000ft) per min**
Service ceiling: **6400m (21,000ft)**	Weight (empty): **5484kg (12,091lb)**
Range: **3154km (1960 miles)**	Weight (loaded): **8845kg (19,500lb)**

LOCKHEED P-38 LIGHTNING

SPECIFICATIONS

LOCKHEED P-38 LIGHTNING

Manufacturer: **Lockheed**	Crew: **One**
Type: **Long-Range Fighter**	Powerplant: **2 x Allison V-1710-111**
Length: **11.53m (37ft 10in)**	Armament: **1 x cannon, 4 x MG**
Span: **15.85m (52ft 0in)**	Bomb load: **1814kg (4000lb)**
Height: **3.91m (12ft 10in)**	First flight: **Not Given**
Maximum speed: **666km/h (414mph)**	Initial climb: **870m (2850ft) per min**
Service ceiling: **13,410m (44,000ft)**	Weight (empty): **5806kg (12,800lb)**
Range: **4184km (2600 miles)**	Weight (loaded): **9798kg (21,600lb)**

In February 1937 the USAAC issued a specification for a long-range interceptor (pursuit) and escort fighter, calling for a speed of 576km/h (360mph) at 6100m (20,000ft) and endurance at this speed of one hour. In response, Lockheed, which had thus far not built a purely military type, created a revolutionary fighter identified as the P-38 that bristled with innovations and posed considerable technical risks.

Powered by two Allison engines, with GEC turbochargers recessed into the tops of twin-tail booms supporting the main units of the tricycle landing gear, and with the pilot seated in the central nacelle behind heavy nose armament and the nosewheel unit, the XP-38 prototype first flew in January 1939. Much development work ensued, and despite mounting costs the aircraft demonstrated such outstanding performance that project funding continued. In August 1941 the initial operational variant, P-38D, entered service and thereafter it saw action in North Africa, northwest Europe and the Pacific. Total production was 9393 aircraft, including conversions to F-4 and F-5 reconnaissance standards. The most important fighter variants, featuring steadily more power, were the P-38E (210), P-38F (527), P-38G (1082), P-38H (601), P-38J (2970) and P-38L (3923). There were also night-fighter, trainer and bomber leader conversions.

LOCKHEED VENTURA

A direct descendant of the Lockheed Model 14, the Model 18 Lodestar first flew in September 1939 and was operated in wartime by the US Army and the RAF. A military aircraft was then developed, which Lockheed offered to the British in coastal reconnaissance and light bomber forms as successor to the Hudson and Bristol Blenheim respectively. The first Ventura Mk I flew on 31 July 1941, and together with the uprated Mk II and Mk IIIA versions entered service in November 1942 in the light bomber role. It proved vulnerable in daylight raids, and during the summer of 1943 was replaced by the Mitchell and Boston. The Ventura was retasked to the maritime role and served with distinction in the Pacific. Later models were the Ventura Mk II and Mk IIA. In American service the Ventura was known as the B-34, and served as bomber trainer (B-34A-2) gunnery trainer (B-34A-3), target tug (B-34A-4), and navigator trainer aircraft. The B-37 was an armed reconnaissance version. The US Navy operated a derivative of the Model 18 transport as the PV Ventura for the patrol bomber role. The core model was the PV-1; 1800 were built and 387 transferred to the UK as Ventura GR.Mk V machines. The US Marine Corps converted a few to night-fighters with British radar equipment, and some PV-1 machines were converted as PV-1P photo-reconnaissance aircraft.

SPECIFICATIONS

LOCKHEED VENTURA

Manufacturer: **Lockheed**	Crew: **Five**
Type: **Coastal Recon' Bomber**	Powerplant: **2 x P & W R-2800-31**
Length: **15.77m (51ft 9in)**	Armament: **6 x MG**
Span: **19.96m (65ft 6in)**	Bomb load: **2268kg (5000lb)**
Height: **3.63m (11ft 11in)**	First flight: **31 July 1941**
Maximum speed: **518km/h (322mph)**	Initial climb: **680m (2230ft) per min**
Service ceiling: **8015m (26,300ft)**	Weight (empty): **9161kg (20,197lb)**
Range: **2671km (1660 miles)**	Weight (loaded): **15,422kg (34,000lb)**

MARTIN B-10B

SPECIFICATIONS

MARTIN B-10B

Manufacturer:
Glenn L. Martin Co.

Crew:
Four

Type:
Medium Bomber

Powerplant:
2 x Wright R-1820

Length:
13.46m (44ft 2in)

Armament:
3 x 0.303in MG

Span:
21.60 m (70ft 10.5in)

Bomb load:
1025kg (2260lb)

Height:
3.53m (11ft 7in)

First flight:
January 1932

Maximum speed:
322km/h (200mph)

Initial climb:
567m (1860ft) per min

Service ceiling:
7680m (25,200ft)

Weight (empty):
4682kg (10,322lb)

Range:
950km (590 miles)

Weight (loaded):
7210kg (15,894lb)

Martin was one of the earliest important suppliers of US Army and Navy aircraft, and in 1922 General Billy Mitchell used Martin MB-2 bombers to demonstrate that battleships could be sunk from the air. After many historic aircraft ventures, Martin built the Model 123 as a company-funded venture and this aircraft may be regarded as one of the most significant advances in the history of military aircraft. It introduced cantilever monoplane wings, flaps, stressed skin construction, retractable landing gear, advanced engine cowls, variable pitch propellers and an internal bomb bay with power-driven doors. It was also the first American warplane to be fitted with turreted armament and despite having only 447kW (600hp) Cyclone engines the prototype was considerably faster than any of the pursuit fighters then in service with the US Army.

The aircraft eventually entered production as the YB-10, for service delivery from June 1934. The US Army Air Corps (USAAC) received 151 examples of the B-10 and B-12 bombers, and had retired all of them before World War II, but some of the aircraft that were exported to China and the Netherlands East Indies in the late 1930s and early 1940s fought against the Japanese, thus becoming the first American-designed bomber to be flown in combat.

MARTIN B-26 MARAUDER

With its established reputation in bomber design and production Martin made concerted efforts to win the 1939 Medium Bomber competition of the US Army, and boldly entered a design featuring a wing optimized for high cruise efficiency rather than landing. This Model 179 was ordered off the drawing board in July 1939 and first flew in November 1940. Production B-26A Marauder aircraft with torpedo shackles between the bomb doors were deployed to Australia the day after the attack on Pearl Harbor, and although inexperienced pilots found the aircraft more than a handful as a result of its high wing loading and high landing speed, once mastered the Marauder was an excellent warplane that achieved good results.

In May 1943 it began its career as the chief medium bomber of the Eighth Air Force in the European theatre, and went on to set a record for the lowest loss rate of any US bomber in Europe. The Marauder was built in a number of variants; the most important were the B-26 (201 machines), B-26A (139 machines with provision for a torpedo), B-26B and identical B-26C (1883 and 1235 machines with uprated engines and, from the 641st model built, a larger vertical tail and increased wing span), and B-26F and essentially similar B-26G (300 and 893 machines with increased wing incidence).

SPECIFICATIONS

MARTIN B-26 MARAUDER

Manufacturer: **Glenn L. Martin Co.**	Crew: **Seven**
Type: **Medium Attack Bomber**	Powerplant: **2 x P & W R-2800-5**
Length: **17.07m (56ft)**	Armament: **4 x 0.50in MG**
Span: **18.81m (65ft)**	Bomb load: **2177kg (4800lb)**
Height: **6.05m (19ft 10in)**	First flight: **25 November 1940**
Maximum speed: **507km/h (315mph)**	Initial climb: **366m (1199ft) per min**
Service ceiling: **7620m (25,000ft)**	Weight (empty): **9696kg (21,375lb)**
Range: **1609km (1000 miles)**	Weight (loaded): **14,515kg (32,000lb)**

NORTH AMERICAN B-25 MITCHELL

SPECIFICATIONS

NORTH AMERICAN B-25 MITCHELL

Manufacturer:
North American Aviation

Type:
(B-25C) Medium Bomber

Length:
16.12m (52ft 11in)

Span:
20.60m (67 ft 7in)

Height:
4.82m (15ft 10in)

Maximum speed:
457km/h (284mph)

Service ceiling:
6460m (21,200ft)

Range:
2454km (1525 miles)

Crew:
Five

Powerplant:
2 x Wright R-2600-13

Armament:
6 x 0.50in MG

Bomb load:
1361kg (3000lb)

First flight:
January 1939

Initial climb:
338m (1100ft) per min

Weight (empty):
9208kg (20,300lb)

Weight (loaded):
18,960kg (41,800lb)

Designed by a team led by Lee Atwood and Ray Rice, the B-25 Mitchell was arguably the best aircraft in its class in World War II and one of the most important US tactical warplanes of the conflict. The origins of the type can be found in the NA-40 of 1938, a company-funded project anticipating that the US Army Air Corps would require a new medium bomber. The NA-40 first flew in January 1939, but was then extensively modified into the sleeker and more powerful NA-40B to meet the definitive USAAC requirement issued in January 1939. The USAAC ordered 184 off the drawing board and received its first B-25 initial production aircraft in February 1941. Later models were the B-25A and B-25B, the former with self-sealing fuel tanks and the latter with dorsal and ventral turrets but no tail gun position.

The B-25B was used in the "Doolittle raid" of April 1942, when 16 aircraft lifted off from an aircraft carrier to bomb Tokyo. Some early concerns were expressed by pilots regarding the type's often tricky handling qualities, but these were soon dispelled and the aircraft began to make a notable impact on the air war. The B-25B was followed into service by the virtually identical B-25C and B-25D, and the heavily armed B-25G and -H anti-shipping models that were evolved for use in the Pacific theatre. In all some 9816 aircraft were completed.

NORTH AMERICAN P-51 MUSTANG

The Mustang is considered to be the best offensive fighter of World War II, and was certainly one of the key elements in the final Allied victory. In April 1940 the British Purchasing Commission concluded an agreement with North American to design and build a new fighter for the RAF. This was completed in a remarkable 117 days, but production of a prototype was held up by the failure of Allison to deliver the chosen engine. The NA-73X finally flew in October 1940 with the Allison V-1710 engine, which was also used in the 1045 examples of the P-51 and P-51A (Mustang Mks I and II) that served from April 1942 in the low-level fighter and reconnaissance-fighter roles. These were indifferent aircraft, but with the installation of the Packard V-1650 (a licence-built copy of the Rolls-Royce Merlin) the Mustang was transformed into one of the most important fighters of the war. The P-51B/C paved the way for the definitive P-51D of which 7966 were completed with a cut-down rear fuselage and clear-view "bubble" canopy, and later with increased fuel capacity and underwing provision for rocket projectiles as alternatives to bombs for the ground-attack role. Later models were the P-51H lightweight model and the P-51K, and the F-6 series of photo-reconnaissance aircraft. With drop tanks, the Mustang units in Britain were able to escort bomber formations all the way to Berlin and back.

SPECIFICATIONS

NORTH AMERICAN P-51 MUSTANG

Manufacturer: **North American Aviation**	Crew: **One**
Type: **Fighter, Fighter-Bomber**	Powerplant: **1 x Packard V-1650-7**
Length: **9.84m (32ft 3.25in)**	Armament: **6 x 0.50in MG**
Span: **11.28m (37ft 0.25in)**	Bomb load: **907kg (2000lb)**
Height: **4.16m (13ft 8in)**	First flight: **26 October 1940**
Maximum speed: **703km/h (437mph)**	Initial climb: **1060m (3475ft) per min**
Service ceiling: **12,770m (41,900ft)**	Weight (empty): **3103kg (6840lb)**
Range: **3703km (2301 miles)**	Weight (loaded): **5493kg (12,100lb)**

REPUBLIC P-43 LANCER

SPECIFICATIONS

REPUBLIC P-43 LANCER

Manufacturer: **Republic Aviation Corp.**	Crew: **One**
Type: **Fighter**	Powerplant: **1 x P & W R-1830-47**
Length: **8.69m (28ft 6in)**	Armament: **4 x MG**
Span: **10.97m (36ft)**	Bomb load: **None**
Height: **4.27m (14ft))**	First flight: **1939**
Maximum speed: **562km/h (349mph)**	Initial climb: **not available**
Service ceiling: **11,580m (38,000ft)**	Weight (empty): **2565kg (5654lb)**
Range: **1287km (800 miles)**	Weight (loaded): **3599kg (7935lb)**

The immediate predecessor to the P-47, and one of the most numerous aircraft in USAAC service in 1941, the P-43 Lancer was evolved from the Seversky P-35 aircraft designed by Alexander Kartveli before the company became Republic Aviation. The last of a production run of 77 P-35s was completed as an improved aircraft and designated XP-41; first flown shortly before the company change of identity, this was fundamentally the prototype of the Republic P-43 Lancer. After extensive testing, Republic completed another improved version and won an order for 13 evaluation aircraft under the designation YP-43. This showed a marked improvement over the P-35, leading in 1940 to a production contract for 54 aircraft (largely to keep the production line open during development of the P-47). The second and last orders were for 80 P-43As, with the more powerful R-1830-49 engine, and 125 P-43A-1s, with a further improved engine.

In 1942 the survivors were converted for use as reconnaissance aircraft as the RP-43, RP-43A and RP-43A-1, and then further modified with different camera installations as the P-43B and P-43C. A number of these were used by the Royal Australian Air Force and Chinese Nationalist forces in the Pacific theatre. The above photograph shows the aircraft in Chinese use.

REPUBLIC P-47 THUNDERBOLT

After analysing the results of air combats in Europe the USAAC set new targets for fighter performance; although he had the replacement for the P-43 already on the drawing board, Republic's chief designer Alexander Kartveli had to start again on the design of a much bigger aircraft to accommodate the new R-2800 engine that such performance demanded. Development was hampered by the difficulty in achieving sufficient ground clearance for the giant 3.65m (12ft) diameter propeller, and by the need to accommodate an inwardly retracting undercarriage and eight guns in the wing.

The XP-47B prototype first flew in May 1941, but only after protracted technical problems had been resolved was it cleared for production. The P-47B Thunderbolt entered service in April 1943, followed by the P-47C fighter-bomber and the definitive P-47D, with an uprated powerplant and, in its major sub-variant, a clear-view "bubble" canopy in place of the original framed canopy and "razorback" rear fuselage. Production of the P-47D and generally similar P-47G "razorback" model totalled 12,603 and 354 respectively. In service the "Jug" (for Juggernaut) was a tough aircraft, able to soak up punishment and dish it out as well. It bore the brunt of early escort duties and was built in larger numbers than any other fighter ever acquired by the USAAC.

SPECIFICATIONS

REPUBLIC P-47 THUNDERBOLT

Manufacturer: **Republic Aviation Corp.**	Crew: **One**
Type: **Fighter, Fighter-Bomber**	Powerplant: **1 x P & W R-2800-59**
Length: **10.99m (36ft 1in)**	Armament: **8 x 0.50in MG**
Span: **12.42m (40ft 9in)**	Bomb load: **1134kg (2500lb)**
Height: **4.44m (14ft 7in)**	First flight: **6 May 1941**
Maximum speed: **700km/h (435mph)**	Initial climb: **855m (2800ft) per min**
Service ceiling: **12,800m (42,000ft)**	Weight (empty): **4858kg (10,700lb)**
Range: **2776km (1725 miles)**	Weight (loaded): **7355kg (16,200lb)**

VOUGHT F4U CORSAIR

SPECIFICATIONS

VOUGHT F4U CORSAIR

Manufacturer:
Chance Vought Aircraft

Crew:
One

Type:
Fighter, Fighter-Bomber

Powerplant:
1 x P & W R-2800-18W

Length:
10.27m (33ft 8.25in)

Armament:
6 x 0.50in MG

Span:
12.49m (40ft 11.75in)

Bomb load:
907kg (2000lb)

Height:
4.50m (14ft 9in)

First flight:
29 May 1940

Maximum speed:
718km/h (446mph)

Initial climb:
1180m (3870ft) per min

Service ceiling:
12,650m (41,500ft)

Weight (empty):
4175kg (9205lb)

Range:
2511km (1560 miles)

Weight (loaded):
8845kg (19,500lb)

Planned by Rex Beisel and Igor Sikorsky to take the most powerful engine and biggest propeller ever fitted to a fighter, even in prototype form the Corsair was the first US warplane to exceed 640km/h (400mph) and outperformed all other American aircraft. The design incorporated an inverted gull-wing to keep span and main landing gear lengths as short as possible, and in original form it had two fuselage and two wing guns. It was later replanned with six 0.50in guns in the outer wings, each with about 490 rounds.

Planned as a carrier-borne fighter the type first flew in May 1940; service deliveries began in July 1942 and it entered operational duties with the US Marine Corps in the Solomons in February 1943, quickly gaining air superiority over the Japanese. Initially it was used only in the land-based role, as it was believed that the aircraft was unsuited to carrier operations. Certainly, the long nose and fearsome torque steer caused more than a few frights, but these were more than outweighed by the aircraft's superlative performance and its abilities in the ground-attack and close-support roles. Armed with bombs and rockets to supplement its fixed guns, the type remained in production until 1952; the main wartime variants were the F4U-1, F4U-4, Goodyear-built FG-1 and the Brewster-built F3A-1 aircraft.

ILYUSHIN Il-2 SHTURMOVIK

Comparable in terms of size, shape, weight and general performance with the Fairey Battle, the Il-2 Shturmovik (Bronirovanni Shturmovik – "armoured attacker") was by far the more successful aircraft and sustained what is known to have been the biggest production run of any aircraft in history. Throughout World War II, production from three large plants averaged about 1200 per month and topped 40,000 aircraft. Designed by the bureau of Sergei Ilyushin as a heavily armoured attack aircraft (with armour accounting for more than 15 per cent of gross weight), the BSh-2 prototype first flew in December 1939 but was found to be underpowered. With the AM-38 subsequent TsKB-57 prototypes were much improved. The type entered service as the single-seat Il-2 in March 1941 and was initially an indifferent warplane with the 1238kW (1660hp) AM-38 engine and an armament of two 20mm cannon and two 7.62mm machine-guns as well as bombs and 82mm rockets. Produced in vast numbers in 1942, it matured into a formidable ground-attack aircraft. The Il-2 was followed by the Il-2M with the AM-38F engine and 23mm cannon, the two-seat Il-2M Tip 3 that had an additional rear-facing crew position for rearward defence, and the Il-2M Tip 3M with 37mm rather than 23mm cannon for greater anti-tank capability.

SPECIFICATIONS

ILYUSHIN Il-2 SHTURMOVIK

Manufacturer: **Ilyushin**	Crew: **Two**
Type: **Close-Support, Anti-Tank**	Powerplant: **1 x Mikulin AM-38F**
Length: **12.00m (39ft 4.5in)**	Armament: **2 x cannon, 3 x MG**
Span: **14.60m (47ft 11in)**	Bomb load: **1000kg (2205lb)**
Height: **3.40m (11ft 1.75in)**	First flight: **30 December 1939**
Maximum speed: **415km/h (258mph)**	Initial climb: **150m (490ft) per min**
Service ceiling: **6000m (19,685ft)**	Weight (empty): **4525kg (9976lb)**
Range: **800km (497 miles)**	Weight (loaded): **6360kg (14,021lb)**

LAVOCHKIN La-5

SPECIFICATIONS

LAVOCHKIN La-5

Manufacturer:
Lavochkin

Crew:
One

Type:
Fighter, Fighter-Bomber

Powerplant:
1 x Shvetsov ASh-82FN

Length:
8.67m (28ft 5.33in)

Armament:
2 x 20mm cannon

Span:
9.80m (32ft 1.75in)

Bomb load:
500kg (1102lb)

Height:
2.54m (8ft 4in)

First flight:
January 1942

Maximum speed:
648km/h (403mph)

Initial climb:
1000m (3280ft) per min

Service ceiling:
11,000m (36,090ft)

Weight (empty):
2605kg (5743lb)

Range:
765km (475 miles)

Weight (loaded):
3402kg (7500lb)

The design bureau led by Semyon Lavochkin produced some of the best fighters for the Soviet air force's fleets during the war. After building the mediocre LaGG-3 in 1939 – accepted largely because it was easy to build – Lavochkin's team in 1941 urgently converted the airframe of one LaGG-3 to accept the Shvetsov M-82 radial engine. The change was ordered in August and the first of several prototypes flew in March 1942. Despite fractionally increased drag, it offered a speed increase to 600km/h (373mph) and, in particular, improved performance at height. The LaGG-3 was cancelled in May 1942, production then switching to the new machine, designated LaG-5. Within a matter of weeks this in turn was replaced on the assembly line by a further improvement, tested as a prototype in early 1942, with a new fuselage containing two 20mm guns and having a lower rear fuselage profile behind a canopy giving all-round vision. In service, this aircraft proved to be 45km/h (28mph) faster than a Bf109G-2 at lower altitude, but the German fighter could outclimb it and efforts were made to reduce its weight. Up to late 1944 some 9920 aircraft were built, in variants such as the La-5 with the 1103.5kW (1480hp) M-82A engine, La-5F with the M-82F (later ASh-82F) engine, definitive La-5FN, and La-5FN Type 41 with a metal rather than wooden wing.

MIKOYAN-GUREVICH MiG-3

In early 1938 the Soviet air force issued a requirement for a modern, high-altitude fighter to replace the Polikarpov I-15. This brought responses from a number of manufacturers, including Yakovlev and the new partnership of Artem I. Mikoyan and Mikhail I. Gurevich. Handicapped by its long and heavy engine, which held the armament to a poor level, the MiG-1 first flew in prototype form in April 1940, its only vice being an extreme tendency to swing on take-off and landing. In view of the amazing rapidity of its development this was an acceptable penalty and production soon got underway.

Some 100 aircraft were built, with an armament of one 12.7mm and two 7.62mm machine-guns, and either open or enclosed accommodation. The type was then replaced in production by the refined MiG-3, with a more powerful engine, new propeller, additional fuel tank, increased dihedral, improved protection and a rearward-sliding rather than side-hinged canopy. Despite adding extra guns on later aircraft it was no match for Luftwaffe fighters and by 1942 the type was being used for armed reconnaissance and close-support, with field modifications allowing the carriage of six RS-82 rockets or two bombs or chemical containers. The production total was 3322 aircraft delivered up to the spring of 1942.

SPECIFICATIONS

MIKOYAN-GUREVICH MiG-3

Manufacturer: **Mikoyan-Gurevich**	Crew: **One**
Type: **Fighter, Fighter-Bomber**	Powerplant: **1 x Mikulin AM-35A**
Length: **8.15m (26ft 9in)**	Armament: **3 x MG**
Span: **10.3m (33ft 9.5in)**	Bomb load: **200kg (441lb)**
Height: **2.61m (8ft 7in)**	First flight: **May 1941**
Maximum speed: **640km/h (398mph)**	Initial climb: **1200m (3937ft) per min**
Service ceiling: **12,000m (39,370ft)**	Weight (empty): **2595kg (5721lb)**
Range: **1195km (742 miles)**	Weight (loaded): **3350kg (7385lb)**

PETLYAKOV Pe-2

SPECIFICATIONS

PETLYAKOV Pe-2

Manufacturer: **Petlyakov**	Crew: **Three**
Type: **Multi-Role Attack Bomber**	Powerplant: **2 x Klimov VK-105RA**
Length: **12.66m (41ft 6.5in)**	Armament: **4 x 7.62mm MG**
Span: **17.16m (56ft 3.7in)**	Bomb load: **1600kg (3527lb)**
Height: **4.00m (13ft 1.5in)**	First flight: **1939**
Maximum speed: **540km/h (335mph)**	Initial climb: **436m (1430ft) per min**
Service ceiling: **8800m (28,870ft)**	Weight (empty): **5870kg (12,943lb)**
Range: **1500km (932 miles)**	Weight (loaded): **8495kg (18,728lb)**

Not until after the war did Western observers begin to appreciate the Pe-2. Built throughout the war, it was one of the outstanding Allied combat aircraft – the Soviet counterpart of the de Havilland Mosquito and Junkers Ju 88. By dint of continual improvement it remained in the front line right up to the German surrender. It was originally planned by Vladimir Petlyakov's team in 1938 as a high-altitude fighter designated VI-100. The prototype flew in 1939–40, but it was then revised as the PB-100 dive-bomber with three rather than two crew in unpressurized accommodation, a powerplant optimized for lower-altitude operations, and different armament. Level bombing at height proved inaccurate, so dive brakes were added and in June 1940 the decision was taken for the PB-100 to be placed in immediate production as the Pe-2 multi-role dive- and attack bomber. This version was supplanted from spring 1942 by the Pe-2FT optimized for fighting with uprated armament, and by replacing the underwing dive brakes with manoeuvre flaps, reduction of the nose glazing and on later aircraft an uprated powerplant. Versions of the Pe-2 were also used for long-range photo-reconnaissance and training. The final Pe-3 multi-purpose fighter version had cannon, machine-guns and underwing provision for rockets. Some 11,427 were built overall.

PETLYAKOV Pe-8

Despite its enormous industrial capacity, and a wealth of highly talented engineers, the Soviet Union was unable to put an effective strategic bomber into production during the war. The only aircraft of this type that entered service was the Petlyakov Pe-8 (identified until 1941 as the Tupolev TB-7). The project began in 1934 with a team led by Vladimir Petlyakov in the design bureau of Andreas Tupolev, who went on to make his name with the medium bombers that served throughout the war. The new aircraft was based on a specification that required optimum performance at a height of 8000m (26,240ft). This requirement proved a constant hindrance, as at the time engines capable of giving sufficient power simply did not exist. The solution was found by fitting four 820kW (1100hp) M-105 engines supercharged by a large blower in the rear fuselage. This was undoubtedly complicated but it worked: in December 1936 it flew and performed brilliantly. This achievement proved unnecessary when it was decided, just as production started in 1939, that the engines should be replaced by AM 35As which did not need the supercharger. It entered service in 1940, but did not make its combat debut until summer 1941; Soviet military planners always placed emphasis on attack aircraft for use in tactical rather than strategic roles.

SPECIFICATIONS

PETLYAKOV Pe-8

Manufacturer: **Tupolev**	Crew: **10**
Type: **Heavy Bomber**	Powerplant: **4 x Mikulin AM-35A**
Length: **22.49m (73ft 9in)**	Armament: **2 x cannon, 3 x MG**
Span: **39.94m (131ft)**	Bomb load: **4000kg (8818lb)**
Height: **6.1m (20ft)**	First flight: **27 December 1936**
Maximum speed: **438km/h (272mph)**	Initial climb: **Not Available**
Service ceiling: **7,065m (22,965ft)**	Weight (empty): **Not Given**
Range: **5,445km (3,383 miles)**	Weight (loaded): **33,325kg (73,469lb)**

POLIKARPOV I-16

SPECIFICATIONS

POLIKARPOV I-16

Manufacturer:
Polikarpov

Crew:
One

Type:
Fighter, Fighter-Bomber

Powerplant:
1 x Shvetsov M-63

Length:
6.13m (20ft 1.3in)

Armament:
4 x 7.62mm MG

Span:
9.00m (29ft 6.33in)

Bomb load:
500kg (1102lb)

Height:
2.57m (8ft 5in)

First flight:
31 December 1933

Maximum speed:
489km/h (304mph)

Initial climb:
850m (2790ft) per min

Service ceiling:
9000m (29,530ft)

Weight (empty):
1490kg (3285lb)

Range:
700km (435 miles)

Weight (loaded):
2095kg (4619lb)

Probably influenced by "Gee-Bee" racers of the United States, Polikarpov's short and simple little I-16 fighter was almost ignored outside the Soviet Union despite the fact that in mass-produced form it was 100–120km/h (60–75mph) faster than fighters elsewhere. Designed in the 1930s alongside the biplane I-15, the I-16 was a more advanced fighter in its basic concept, with a wooden monocoque body, metal/fabric wing and variable pitch propeller. It was also the USSR's first cantilever lo-wing monoplane fighter to feature retractable main landing gear units (although the gear had to be retracted by pumping a handle 100 times!). It first flew in December 1933, revealing tricky handling characteristics – a result of its mounting a radial engine in a short fuselage. Even so it entered large-scale production (7005 aircraft excluding about 1640 two-seat trainers). It came to the fore with the Republicans in Spain where its reliability, manoeuvrability and fast climb and dive surprised opponents who called it the "Rata" (Rat). It then served against the Japanese over China and continued to be flown heroically against far superior opposition until 1942, when increasing losses forced its withdrawal. It was produced in 10 main variants between the I-16 Tip 1 with the 358kW (480hp) M-22 radial and the definitive I-16 Tip 24 with more engine power and armament.

COMMONWEALTH WIRRAWAY

In 1936 the Australian government decided to embark on a programme to create a national aircraft industry that could eventually make Australia independent of imports, and created the Commonwealth Aircraft Corporation in Melbourne. CAC's first product was the CA-1 Wirraway, which was the Australian version of the North American NA-33, an improved version of the NA-26 advanced trainer produced for the USAAC as the BC-1. The first of two CA-1 prototypes flew in March 1939, paving the way for the Wirraway Mk I of which 755 were built in seven blocks during World War II with the factory designations CA-1 to CA-16.

The type entered service in June 1939. However, the Wirraway was by no means a combat aircraft, and when Australia suddenly found itself in the Pacific front line in December 1941 it had no modern fighters, save for a few Brewster Buffaloes supplied to the RAAF in Singapore, so Commonwealth decided to build its own, resulting in the Commonwealth Boomerang. As a result of the good performance and useful armament offered by the Wirraway it was pressed into limited operational service during 1942 in numerous roles including bomber, fighter, ground-attack plane and reconnaissance-mount, all of which it carried out with surprising effectiveness thanks to its enterprising crews.

SPECIFICATIONS

COMMONWEALTH WIRRAWAY

Manufacturer: **Commonwealth Aircraft**	Crew: **Two**
Type: **(CA-3) Trainer**	Powerplant: **1 x P & W R-1340S1H**
Length: **8.48m (27ft 10in)**	Armament: **3 x 0.303in MG**
Span: **13.10m (43ft)**	Bomb load: **None**
Height: **3.7m (12ft)**	First flight: **27 March 1939**
Maximum speed: **354km/h (220mph)**	Initial climb: **Not Available**
Service ceiling: **7000m (23,000ft)**	Weight (empty): **1811kg (3992lb)**
Range: **1150km (720 miles)**	Weight (loaded): **2991kg (6595lb)**

INDEX